Sue Kay & Vaughan Jones

Inside Out

Student's
Book

Elementary

MACMILLAN

0 Classroom

On the whiteboard:

d) pen = e) something you use to write with
f) There's a pen on my desk.
g) Is it a red pen?
h) No, it isn't.

Lexis: the classroom

1 Work with a partner. Match the objects in the picture with the words in the box.

> the board   a word   an answer   a bag   a book   the cassette player
> a chair   a definition   a desk   a dictionary   the door   a map   a pen
> a picture   a piece of paper   a question   a sentence   a student
> the teacher   a window

For example: *a) = a picture   b) = a window*

2 01 Listen, check and repeat the words in 1.

3 02 Listen and point to things in your classroom.

4 Work with a partner. Point to things in your classroom. Ask and answer questions.

For example: *A: What's that in English?*
                     B: A picture.
                     B: What's this in English.
                     A: A pen.

5 Draw a picture of your classroom and label it.

LANGUAGE TOOLBOX

What's this?

What's that?

Lexis: teacher language

1 Work with a partner. Complete each teacher instruction with a word from the box.

> ~~Work~~   Use   Write   Look   Read   Listen

a) *Work* <u>with a partner</u>.

b) ____ at the <u>board</u>.

c) ____ to the <u>conversation</u>.

d) ____ <u>the answers</u> on a piece of paper.

e) ____ the <u>text</u>.

f) ____ <u>your dictionary</u>.

2 🔲 **03** Listen and check your answers in 1.

3 Work with a partner. Make more teacher instructions. Replace the <u>underlined</u> words in 1 with words from the box.

> ~~in groups of three~~   article   song   photograph   a piece of paper
> your name

For example: *Work in groups of three.*

Lexis: student language

1 🔲 **04** Read and listen to the conversation. Put the pictures in the correct order.

Student A: How do you say *compañero* in English?
Teacher: 'Partner'
Student A: How do you spell it?
Teacher: P-A-R-T-N-E-R
Student A: Can you repeat that?
Teacher: P-A-R-T-N-E-R
Student A: Okay … You're my partner.
Student B: Uh … I don't understand.
Student A: You - are - my - partner.
Student B: What does 'partner' mean?
Student A: 'Compañero'!

2 Work in groups of three.

- Practise saying the student language in the conversation in 1.
- Act out the conversation.

Lina

Kate

Mike

1 *You*

Listening (1)

1 Mike wants to join the Sportica Health Club. Complete the questions Lina asks Mike with *you* or *your*.

a) What's *your* first name?
b) What's _____ surname?
c) Where do _____ live?
d) What's _____ telephone number?
e) How old are _____ ?
f) What do _____ do?
g) Are _____ married?
h) What are _____ interested in?

2 📼 **05** Listen to the conversation and check your answers to 1.

3 📼 **06** Listen to the questions in 1 again and practise saying them.

4 Find out information about people in the class. Use questions from 1.

PERSONAL DETAILS	
FIRST NAME	Mike
SURNAME	Turnbull
ADDRESS	23 Trinity Road, London SW18
PHONE	09732 176 773
AGE	27
OCCUPATION	Engineer
MARITAL STATUS	single / married
INTERESTS	gym aerobics swimming yoga tennis squash boxing tai chi

Listening (2)

1 Kate wants to find out information about Mike. Complete the questions Kate asks Lina with *he* or *his*.

a) What's *his* name?
b) Where does _____ live?
c) What's _____ telephone number?
d) How old is _____ ?
e) What does _____ do?
f) Is _____ married?

2 📼 **07** Listen to the conversation and check your answers to 1. In which order does Kate ask the questions?

1 *a*	2 *e*	3	4	5	6

3 Find out how much information your partner knows about people in the class. Use questions from 1.

For example:
'What's her name?' 'Paula'.
'Where does she live?' 'I don't know.'
'What does she do?' '…'

Name & number

Alphabet   **1** 🔊 **08** Say the letters *A E I O U*. Add each letter to an appropriate sound group in the table. Listen, check and repeat the answers.

/eɪ/ face	/i:/ green	/e/ ten	/aɪ/ eye	/əʊ/ nose	/u:/ blue	/ɑ:/ start
[A] H J K	B C D ☐ G P T V	F L M N S X Z	☐ Y	☐	Q ☐ W	R

2 🔊 **09** Listen and write down the order in which you hear the following groups.

a) A E I O U   b) A I O E U   c) E I A U O *1*   d) I A O U E   e) I U A O E

3 Work with a partner. Student A look at page 86. Student B look at page 98.

4 🔊 **10** Listen and write down some well-known abbreviations. Match each abbreviation to its meaning in the box.

> ~~Unidentified Flying Object~~   Very Important Person   Cable News Network
> United Nations   International Olympic Committee   Central Intelligence Agency
> International Business Machines   British Broadcasting Corporation

For example: *1 UFO = Unidentified Flying Object*

5 Are any of these abbreviations different in your language? What other abbreviations do you know? What do they mean?

Spelling   **1** 🔊 **11** Listen to Lina checking the spelling of some new Sportica club members. <u>Underline</u> the correct spelling.

a) <u>Stewart</u> / Stuart   c) Graham / Graeme
b) Clare / Claire   d) Kathryn / Catherine

2 🔊 **12** Here are some more names that have two different spellings but the same pronunciation. Listen and repeat the names after the recording.

a) Alison / Alyson   c) Jill / Gill   e) Lesley / Leslie
b) Jeff / Geoff   d) Lawrence / Laurence   f) Stephen / Steven

3 Work with a partner. Use the names in 2 and copy the conversations in 1. Take it in turns to be Lina.

Lina: What's your name?
Person: ____
Lina: Is that _____ ?
Person: No, it's _____
Lina: Okay, thanks.

Telephone numbers   **1** 🔊 **13** How do you say the telephone numbers in *UK travel – useful numbers*? Listen and check your answers.

2 Work with a partner. Complete the following task.

- Write the names of three people you know with their telephone numbers.
- Dictate the names and numbers to your partner.
- Check that the names and numbers your partner has are correct.

UK TRAVEL   USEFUL NUMBERS

Heathrow flights:
0870 000 0123

UK train times:
0845 748 4950

National Express buses:
0870 580 8080

Hertz Car Rental:
020 8897 2072

British Tourist Authority:
020 8846 9000

Favourites

Lexis

1 Complete the table about singer Enrique Iglesias' favourite things. Use words from the box.

~~Sport~~	Food	Month	Writer	Drink	Actor	City	Day	Car	Colour

Enrique's FAVOURITE THINGS

Sport:	Football	____ :	Coke
____ :	Keanu Reeves, Meryl Streep	____ :	Jeep
____ :	Ernest Hemingway	____ :	Friday
____ :	Black, white, grey, red	____ :	May
____ :	Sushi	____ :	Madrid, Miami, Mexico City

2 Work with a partner. Use the ten headings in 1 and categorise the items in the box.

> January   blue   April   coffee   Thursday   Agatha Christie   June
> pasta   yellow   London   Monday   Robert de Niro   September
> BMW   Wednesday   tea   December   water   golf   Tuesday
> November   Gabriel García Márquez   July   Sunday   Fiat   skiing
> hamburgers   February   Saturday   Julia Roberts   tennis   October
> Paris   August   Toyota   basketball   March   green

3 Underline or add your own favourite item for each category in 2.

4 Choose five categories from 2. For each category, ask *Yes/No* questions to find someone with the same favourite as you.

> For example: *'Is your favourite colour red?' 'Yes, it is.'*
> *'Is your favourite actor Brad Pitt?' 'No, it isn't. It's …'*

Close up

**Questions &
short answers**

Language reference p9

Verb structures p114

1 Work with a partner. For each question write two possible answers.

a)	Are you Spanish?	*Yes, I am.*	*No, I'm not.*
b)	Do you live near here?	*Yes, I do.*	*No, I don't.*
c)	Have you got any brothers and sisters?	*Yes, I have.*	*No, I haven't.*
d)	Are you married?	____	____
e)	Do you like Italian food?	____	____
f)	Have you got a motorbike?	____	____
g)	Do you like watching television?	____	____

2 🔊 14 Listen, check and repeat. Work with a partner. Ask and answer the questions in 1. Discuss your answers.

3 Work with a partner. Complete each question below in three different ways. Use words and expressions provided or your own ideas.

a) Are you (hungry?   tired?   happy?   stressed?   nervous?   ____ ?)
b) Do you like (dancing?   karaoke?   beer?   swimming?   skiing?   ____ ?)
c) Do you (smoke?   speak French?   live with your parents?   drive?   ____ ?)
d) Have you got (a bicycle?   a computer?   a pet?   a mobile phone?   ____ ?)

4 Use your questions from 3. Interview another person in the class.

Language reference: questions & short answers

You use *be*, *do* or *have* to make questions and give short answers.

	Question	Short answer *Yes*	Short answer *No*
be:	*Are you married?*	*Yes, I am.*	*No, I'm not (I am not).*
do:	*Do you speak French?*	*Yes, I do.*	*No, I don't (I do not).*
have:	*Have you got a car?*	*Yes, I have.*	*No, I haven't (I have not).*

She's Got You

1 Match the pictures with the words in the box. Which things do you think it is usual for a man to give to a woman when they are in love?

> a penknife   a picture   golf clubs   a bicycle   records   a memory
> a pen   a class ring

2 [cassette] 15 Listen to the song, *She's Got You*, look at the picture and answer the questions. (The tapescript is on page 119.)

a) Which things in 1 has the singer got?
b) What has the other woman got?
c) Do you think the singer feels: *happy; sad; angry*?

She's Got You

Released in 1962, this was one of Country singer, Patsy Cline's most popular songs.

The singer (*I*)   The man (*You*)   The other woman (*She*)

3 What objects remind you of people, things or events? Complete this sentence in three ways that are true for you: *When I hear/see … I think of …* Discuss your sentences with a partner.

For example: *When I see a white cat I think of my pet, Snowy.*
When I hear the sea I think of summer holidays with my family.

2 People

Lexis: family words

1 Read the description of the two Tait families. Name each person in the photograph.

LANGUAGE TOOLBOX

have got

I've got – I have got
you've got – you have got
he's got – he has got
she's got – she has got
it's got – it has got
we've got – we have got
they've got – they have got

Regular plurals

1 son – 2 sons
1 family – 2 families

Irregular plurals

1 person – 2 people
1 child – 2 children
1 man – 2 men
1 woman – 2 women

Meet the Taits

CHARLIE TAIT AND WILLIE TAIT are identical twin brothers. Charlie is married to Lisa, and Willie is married to Dawn. Lisa and Dawn are sisters. Both couples have got three children. Charlie and Lisa have got one son and two daughters. Kevin is 16, Kylie is 13, and Claire is 6. Willie and Dawn have got two sons and one daughter. Michael is 16, Scott is 12, and Becky is 5. The two families live next door to each other in Newcastle.

2 Work with a partner. Read the following descriptions and identify the people.

1	**2**	**3**	**4**	**5**
Charlie is my **father**. Lisa is my **mother**. I've got two **sisters** called Kylie and Claire.	Charlie is her **uncle**. Lisa is her **aunt**. She's got two **brothers**.	Dawn is his **sister-in-law**. Michael and Scott are his **nephews**. He's got one **niece**.	Kevin, Kylie and Claire are our **cousins**. Willie and Dawn are our **parents**. We've got a little **sister** called Becky.	Kevin is their **nephew**. Kylie and Claire are their **nieces**. They've got two **sons** and a **daughter**.
Who am I? *Kevin*	Who is she?	Who is he?	Who are we?	Who are they?

3 Write a similar description for Kylie, Lisa or Claire from the photo. Give it to your partner. Who is it?

4 Work with a partner. Student A look at page 86. Student B look at page 98.

5 Work with a partner. Describe the family of one of your aunts or uncles.

For example: *My Uncle Sven is married to Ulrika. They've got three children. Their son's name is …*

What do you do?

Lexis: jobs **1** Work with a partner. Match the pictures with the different jobs in the box.

a nurse   an engineer   a DJ   a secretary   a mechanic   a student

 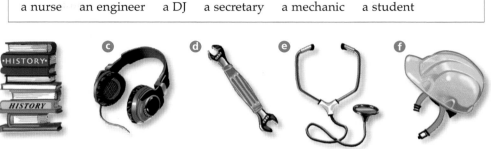

LANGUAGE TOOLBOX

Present simple
I talk
you talk
he talks
she talks
it talks
we talk
they talk

---

2 Complete the following with *a/an* and *in/for*.

a) My mother is *a* nurse. She works *in* a hospital.
b) My father is ____ engineer. He works ____ a big construction company.
c) My cousin is ____ DJ. He works ____ a night club.
d) My friend is ____ secretary. She works ____ an office.
e) My uncle is ____ mechanic. He works ____ his father.

3 ▭ **16** Listen, check and repeat the answers to 2.

4 Make the sentences in 2 true for your mother, your father, your cousin, etc.

Close up

Present simple

(Language reference p12)

(Verb structures p114)

1 ▭ **17** Complete the conversation with words from the box. Listen and check.

does   Has   ~~Is~~   doesn't   hasn't   isn't   Does   Is

Beth: This is me with my brother.
Angie: Oh, he's nice. (1) *Is* he married?
Beth: No, he (2) ____ . He's single.
Angie: (3) ____ he got a girlfriend?
Beth: No, he (4) ____ .
Angie: Oh. What (5) ____ he do?
Beth: He's a doctor.
Angie: Oh. (6) ____ he live near here?
Beth: No, he (7) ____ . He lives in Australia, actually.
Angie: Oh. (8) ____ this your father?
Beth: No, that's my boyfriend.
Angie: Oh, sorry.

2 Who are the people in the picture?

3 Complete these *Yes/No* questions and short answers with the correct auxiliary verbs.

a) *Are* you a student at university?   *Yes, I am.*   *No, I'm not.*
b) ____ you got a part-time job?   *Yes,* ____   *No,* ____
c) ____ you work in an office?   ____   ____
d) ____ your grandfather retired?   ____   ____
e) ____ your father got an interesting job?   ____   ____
f) ____ your mother speak English?   ____   ____
g) ____ you play the piano?   ____   ____
h) ____ your grandmother live near you?   ____   ____

4 ▭ **18** Listen, check and repeat. Work with a partner. Ask and answer the questions in 3. Discuss your answers.

Language reference: present simple

You use *do* or *does* to make questions and give short answers with all verbs (except *be* and *have got*) in the present simple.

Question	Short answer *Yes*	Short answer *No*
Do you live in London?	*Yes, I do.*	*No, I don't (I do not).*
Does he work in an office?	*Yes, he does.*	*No, he doesn't (he does not).*
Do they like coffee?	*Yes, they do.*	*No, they don't (they do not).*

Note: You don't use *do* or *does* with *be* or *have got*.
'Are you retired?' NOT ~~Do you be retired?~~
'Has your sister got a job?' NOT ~~Does your sister have got a job?~~

Family

Listening   **1**   ▭ **19** Listen to Beth talking about more members of her family. Which two pictures does she talk about?

2   Make sentences about Amy and Robert from the words and phrases in the box. Listen again and compare your sentences with the recording.

> **Amy:** ~~city centre~~   ~~baby boy~~   lovely   teacher   school
> **Robert**: San Francisco   actor   waiter   Italian restaurant   every year

For example: *She lives in the city centre.   She's got a baby boy.*

Possessive -'s   **1**   Work with a partner. Say who each person on the family tree is in relation to Beth.

For example: *Terry is Beth's grandfather. June is Beth's grandmother.* etc.

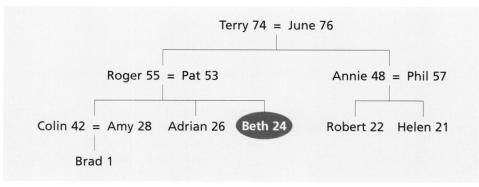

2   Draw your family tree. Ask and answer questions about your partner's family.

> Who?   Where ... live?   Married?   What ... do?   *etc.*

Anecdote **1** 🔲 20 Think about one of your relatives. You are going to tell your partner about him or her. Read and listen to the questions and think about your answers.

☐ Is it a man or a woman?   It's a …

☐ What's his or her name?   His/Her name's …

☐ What relation is he or she to you?   He/She's my … (mother, grandfather, brother, cousin, etc.)

☐ Where does he or she live?   He/She lives in …

☐ What does he or she do?   He/She's … (a teacher, a sales manager, a student, retired, etc.)

☐ Is he or she married?   He/She's … (married, single, etc.)

☐ Has he or she got children?   He/She's got …

☐ What do you do and what do you talk about when you see him or her?   We …

2 Think about what to say and how to say it. Use the sentence beginnings to help you.

3 Tell your partner about your relative.

International relations

Word stress **1** Work with a partner. Copy and complete the table with the correct words. Say each word and <u>underline</u> the stressed syllable.

Flag	Country 'I come from …'	Nationality 'I am …'	Language 'I speak …'	Flag	Country 'I come from …'	Nationality 'I am …'	Language 'I speak …'
	Argentina	Argentinian	Spanish	●	Japan	(5) ____	Japanese
	Brazil	(1) ____	Portuguese		(6) ____	Polish	Polish
	France	French	(2) ____		Spain	(7) ____	Spanish
	(3) ____	German	German		the United Kingdom	British	(8) ____
	Italy	Italian	(4) ____		the (9) ____	American	English

2 🔲 21 Listen, check and repeat your answers. Add more countries to your table.

3 Write the names of people you know from different countries. (You can include TV and film stars if you wish.) Tell your partner about them.

For example: *Eva is Polish. She's from Kracow. She lives in Warsaw. She's married and she's got three children. She works for a publishing company.*

Enrique Iglesias is Spanish. He's from Madrid. He lives in Miami. He isn't married. He's a famous international singer.

3 Days

Lexis: daily activities

1 Work with a partner. Complete the table by matching the verbs (*watch, do, have, go, listen to*) with the nouns to make ten different daily activities.

a) *do*	b) ____	c) ____	d) ____	e) ____
• the washing up • the ironing	• to the park • for a walk	• a cup of tea • lunch with friends	• the radio • the birds singing	• television • films and sport

2 🔲 **22** You are going to listen to eight people (*1–8*) saying what they do when they want to relax. Check your answers to 1.

3 Listen again and add one more activity to each column. Which of the daily activities in the table do you do? Compare with your partner.

Reading

Suzanne Vega
New York singer-songwriter. Hits include *Luka* and *Tom's Diner*.

1 Work with a partner. You are going to read about Suzanne Vega's perfect day in New York. Match a verb from column A with an appropriate phrase from column B.

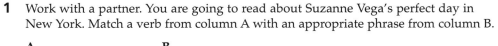

A		B
1	get up	with my friends
2	go for a	sailing
3	watch	the newspaper
4	have	drink
5	go out	late
6	read	breakfast
7	go	the people walk by

2 Work with a partner and complete the following tasks.

a) Match each of the pictures below with at least one of the activities in 1.
b) Read the article and put the pictures in the correct order.
c) What is your 'perfect day'? Tell your partner.

ON A PERFECT DAY IN NEW YORK

I get up late, not before 10.30 or 11 o'clock. I read *The New York Times* for about an hour. Then I have breakfast at *Le Gamin*. I have a croissant and a big bowl of their coffee and chocolate mixture and finish reading the newspaper. In the afternoon I go sailing on the lake in Central Park.

At about five o'clock I go for a drink at the restaurant in Central Park. I sit and watch the people walk by. In the evening, I go out with my friends. Where? Who knows. You can do anything in New York.

1 ▪️ **23** Listen and repeat the verbs in the box. Put each verb in the correct column in the table.

~~acts~~ finishes laughs needs pays relaxes takes teaches wins

Ending with /s/	Ending with /z/	Ending with /ɪz/
acts		

2 ▪️ **24** Listen, check and repeat the answers to 1.

3 ▪️ **25** Complete these chants with verbs from the table in 1. Listen, check and repeat the answers.

'I cry, he (1) *laughs*.'   'I want, she needs.'   'I learn, she (5) ____ .'
'I give, she (2) ____ .'   'I spend, he (3) ____ .'   'I work, he relaxes.'
'I think, he acts.'   'I lose, she (4) ____ .'   'I start, she (6) ____ .'
'We're different.'   'We're different.'   'We're married!'

'I cry, he laughs.'

Close up

Adverbs of frequency

1 Work with a partner. Compare yourself to Suzanne Vega. Ask the questions and use phrases in the box to answer.

For example: *'Do you ever get up after 11am?' 'No, never.'*

a) 'Do you ever get up after 11am?'
b) 'Do you ever have breakfast in a restaurant?'
c) 'Do you ever read the newspaper after breakfast?'
d) 'Do you ever go sailing in the afternoon?'
e) 'Do you ever go for a drink at about five o'clock?'
f) 'Do you ever go out with your friends in the evening?'

'Yes, always.'   100%
'Yes, usually.'   ▲
'Yes, often.'
'Yes, sometimes.'
'No, hardly ever.'   ▼
'No, never.'   0%

2 Work with a partner. Student A look at page 86. Student B look at page 98.

3 Complete the following sentences with *in*, *on* or *at*.

a) Something you never do *on* Sundays.
b) Something you always do ____ the morning.
c) Something you usually do ____ the weekend.
d) Something you often do ____ your birthday.
e) Something you sometimes do ____ Saturday nights.
f) Something you usually do ____ summer.

4 Write true sentences about the ideas in 3. Compare your sentences with a partner.

For example: *I never get up before 10am on Sundays.*

Language reference: adverbs of frequency

always   usually   often   sometimes   hardly ever   never
100% ————————————————————➤ 0%

Adverbs of frequency usually go before the main verb, but after the verb *be*.

          adverb   verb
*I **hardly ever** get up after 11am.*

                    adverb   verb
*Does he **often** buy you presents?*

          be   adverb
*She's **sometimes** late for the lesson.*

A day in the life of ...

Reading

1 Look at the two photographs and read the sentences. Which person does each sentence describe? <u>Underline</u> *He* or *She*.

a) He/She lives in the country.
b) He/She never has breakfast.
c) He/She listens to reggae in the morning.
d) He/She never goes to the gym.
e) He/She drinks a lot of water.
f) He/She trains for two hours every morning.
g) He/She has meat, fish and vegetables for lunch.
h) He/She does the housework in the afternoon.
i) He/She doesn't drink alcohol.
j) He/She loves roast dinners and chocolate.

2 Read the article and check your answers to 1.

LITTLE AND
LARGE

Jodie Kidd became a model when she was 15. She doesn't like cities. She lives in the country with her horses, dogs, cats and chickens. She never goes to the gym, but she really likes sports, especially polo and swimming. She also goes riding every day. She doesn't smoke and she doesn't drink alcohol. But she loves roast dinners and chocolate. She often visits her parents in their home in Barbados.

Musashimaru weighs more than 225 kilograms and is a grand champion of sumo wrestling. He lives at the Musashigawa 'stable' in Tokyo with thirty other wrestlers. 'I always wake up before 7am, make my bed and listen to reggae. I never have breakfast. I train for two hours, then I have a shower. After training, I always drink a lot of water. For lunch I have meat, fish and vegetables. In the afternoon I sometimes have a nap or I sometimes go for a walk. At three o'clock in the afternoon we do the housework. In the evening I usually go out to a restaurant for a Chinese, Italian or sushi. I go home at 11.30pm.

3 Work with a partner. Ask each other questions and re-write the sentences in 1 so that they are true for your partner.

For example: *'Cibele, do you live in the country?' 'No, I don't.'*
Cibele doesn't live in the country.

Lexis: *make & do*

1 Add *make* or *do* to the appropriate diagram to form common expressions.

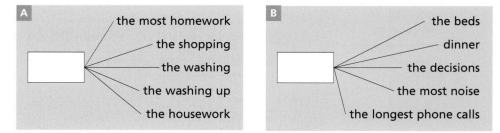

2 At home, who makes or does the things in 1? Make sentences and compare with your partner.

For example: *My mum does the housework. My brother makes the most noise. I do the most homework.*

Love it. Hate it.

Listening **1** Complete the key with words from the box. You can use words more than once.

~~love~~   like   mind   hate   don't   really

♥☺	👍☺	☺	😐	😞	😞👎
KEY: a) I *love* it	b) I ____ ____ it	c) I ____ it	d) I ____ ____ it	e) I ____ ____ it	f) I ____ it

2 Read about Jack and Layla. Are you similar to Jack or similar to Layla?

Jack loves water, really likes being outside, really likes sport, hates towns and cities and doesn't like loud music.

Layla loves spending money, doesn't like being outside, hates doing housework but doesn't mind cooking, likes dancing but hates sport.

3 🎞 26 Work with a partner. Look at the activities in the box. Put *J* if you think Jack likes it. Put *L* if you think Layla likes it. Listen and check your answers.

playing football   shopping   swimming   clubbing   jogging eating out in restaurants   going to the gym   going to rock concert

Close up

Likes & dislikes **1** Match the questions with the answers.

LANGUAGE TOOLBOX
Pronouns
Subject   **Object**
I   me
you   you
he   him
she   her
it   it
we   us
they   them

a) Do you like camping?
b) Do you like Pavarotti?
c) Do you like cats?
d) Do you like Madonna?
e) Does your boss/teacher like you?

1 No, I hate them.
2 Yes, I think he likes me.
3 Yes, I love it.
4 Yes, I like him a lot.
5 She's okay. I don't mind her.

2 Make the answers in 1 true for you and compare with your partner.

3 Work with a partner. Complete the table to show the spelling of the *-ing* form.

Verbs ending in *-e*	Verbs ending in 1 vowel + 1 consonant	Other verbs
dance → *dancing* write → ____ phone → ____	swim → *swimming* shop → ____ jog → ____	read → *reading* cook → ____ draw → ____

4 Work with a partner. Student A look at page 87. Student B look at page 99.

Language reference: likes & dislikes

♥☺   👍☺   ☺   😐   😞   😞👎
love   *really like*   *like*   *don't mind*   *don't like*   *hate*

Verbs to show likes and dislikes always take an object. The object can be a noun, a pronoun or an *-ing* form.

subject	verb	object
I	*love*	*football.* (noun)
He	*likes*	*it.* (pronoun)
She	*hates*	*doing the housework.* (*-ing* form)

4 Living

Reading

1 Look at the photographs below. Which one is a real royal palace? What do you know about it?

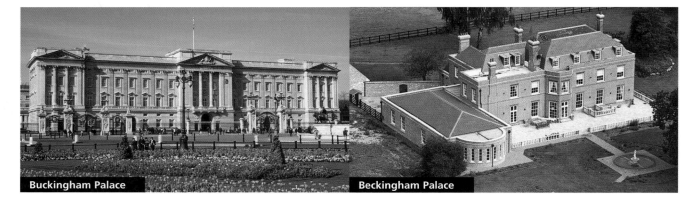

Buckingham Palace   Beckingham Palace

2 Match the two articles below with the photographs in 1. Complete the texts with Beckingham or Buckingham.

____ Palace was built in 1703. It is situated in the centre of London. Queen Elizabeth II lives and works there most of the time. She invites more than 50,000 guests to the palace every year. In August and September the Queen stays in Scotland, and part of the palace is open to the public.

'____ Palace' was built in 1930 and belongs to the Beckham family. Victoria Beckham (Posh Spice) was a member of a pop group called the Spice Girls. She is married to England football player, David Beckham. They have two children. At their wedding reception in Ireland they sat on red and gold thrones. After that, the press named their house '____ Palace'.

3 Read the articles again. Are the following statements true or false?

a) Buckingham Palace is in Scotland.
b) Queen Elizabeth II lives in Buckingham Palace all year.
c) Tourists can only visit Buckingham Palace in August and September.
d) David and Victoria Beckham got married in Ireland.
e) They named their house 'Beckingham Palace'.

4 Work with a partner. Read the following information. Which sentences do you think describe Beckingham Palace and which ones describe Buckingham Palace?

a) There's a recording studio.
b) There's a bathroom dedicated to the actress, Audrey Hepburn.
c) There are 609 rooms.
d) There's a children's playroom.
e) There are paintings by Rembrandt, Rubens and Vermeer.
f) There's an indoor swimming pool.
g) There's a ballroom.
h) There's a throne room.

5 Work with a partner. Student A turn to page 87 and read the rest of the article about Beckingham Palace. Student B turn to page 99 and read the rest of the article about Buckingham Palace. Check your answers to 4.

6 What things in Beckingham or Buckingham Palace would you like in your house?

Lexis: rooms

1 Look at the photo of a living room. <u>Underline</u> the things in the box that you can see.

> <u>armchair</u> bath bed
> blinds *or* curtains
> bookcase carpet *or* rug
> coffee table cooker
> cupboard cushions
> dishwasher fireplace
> fridge lamp mirror
> picture plant radiator
> shelf/shelves shower
> sink sofa stereo
> television toilet
> wardrobe washbasin
> washing machine

2 Work with a partner. Which things in the box in 1 can you usually find in:
a) a kitchen; b) a bedroom; or c) a bathroom?

3 🔲 27 Listen and check your answers to 2. Repeat the words.

Lexis: prepositions (1)

1 Work with a partner. Rearrange the beginnings and ends of these sentences to make true statements about the photo above.

a) There's a red cushion *on the floor.*
b) There's a lamp *above the sofa.*
c) There's a rug *on the armchair.*
d) There's a magazine *in the corner.*
e) There are some white cushions *next to the sofa.*
f) There are some pictures *under the coffee table.*
g) There's a radiator *on the sofa.*

2 Think about the things in your home. Complete the following sentences to make them true for you. Compare your sentences with a partner.

a) There are *(1, 2, 3, etc.)* clocks. d) There are ____ plants.
b) There are ____ mirrors. e) There are ____ pictures.
c) There are ____ phones. f) There are ____ lamps.

3 Work with a partner. Explain the exact location of the things in 2 in your home.

For example: *There are three clocks. There's one … . There's one … , and there's one … .*

Close up

there is / there are

[Language reference p20]

1 Work with a partner. Complete the questions and write two possible answers.

a) *Is there a fireplace in your living room?* *Yes, there is.* *No, there isn't.*
b) ____ there any posters on your bedroom walls? *Yes, there are.* *No, ____ .*
c) ____ there any plants in your kitchen? ____ ____
d) ____ there a carpet on your bathroom floor? ____ ____
e) ____ there ____ park near your home? ____ ____
f) ____ there ____ good shops near your home? ____ ____

2 🔲 28 Listen, check and repeat. Work with a partner. Ask and answer the questions in 1. Discuss your answers.

3 Work with a partner. Student A look at page 87. Student B look at page 99.

Where do you want to live?

Lexis: prepositions (2)

1 Answer questions *1–4* in the article. Compare your answers with a partner.

2 Work with your partner. Read and complete the horoscopes with appropriate prepositions. How accurate is your horoscope description?

in the city   on a hill   by the sea   near a river   next to a lake

Your house in the stars

★1 Do you like living in a house or would you prefer to be on the top floor of a modern block of flats?

★2 Do you like living in the city, or would you prefer to live on a hill in the country?

★3 Do you want to be in the mountains or by the sea?

★4 Do you want to be near a river or next to a lake?

Apparently, it all depends on your star sign.

Capricorn
22nd Dec. – 19th Jan.
You want to live
(1) ____ a small village
(2) ____ the mountains.

Aquarius
20th Jan. – 17th Feb.
You want to live (3) ____
a big house (4) ____ a hill
with a lot of light.

Pisces
18th Feb. – 19th Mar.
You're happy when you're
(5) ____ the sea.

Aries
20th Mar. – 19th Apr.
You love living (6) ____ the
city because you want to
be (7) ____ the shops.

Taurus
20th Apr. – 20th May
You'd like to have two
homes: a flat (8) ____ the
city and a weekend house
(9) ____ the country.

Gemini
21st May – 20th Jun.
You can't decide! You like
living (10) ____ the city,
but you also   like
being (11) ____ the country
or (12) ____ the sea.

Cancer
21st Jun. – 22nd Jul.
You love water – you want
a house (13) ____ a lake or
a river.

Leo
23rd Jul. – 22nd Aug.
You want to be (14) ____
a big house (15) ____ a
hot country.

Virgo
23rd Aug. – 22nd Sep.
You want to live (16) ____
the top floor of a modern
flat (17) ____ a nice, clean
part of town.

Libra
23rd Sep. – 22nd Oct.
You want a beautiful house
(18) ____ a lake (19) ____
the country.

Scorpio
23rd Oct. – 21st Nov.
You want to leave the city
and live (20) ____ an island.

Sagittarius
22nd Nov. – 21st Dec.
You like the city and the
country, so you want to
live (21) ____ the city
(22) ____ a park.

3 Work in small groups. Discuss the questions.

a) Do you agree with the description for your star sign?
b) Do you usually read your horoscope in magazines?
c) Are your horoscope predictions usually accurate?

1 📼 **29** Think about your home. You are going to tell your partner about it. Read and listen to the statements and questions and think about your answers.

> ☐ You are walking to your home. Are you in the city or the country?
> ☐ You are in front of your home. Is it a house or a flat? Is it old or modern?
> ☐ What colour is the front door? Is there a number on it? What is the number?
> ☐ You open the door and go inside. What can you see?
> ☐ You go into the kitchen. Is it light or dark? What is there in the kitchen?
> ☐ You go into the living room. Is it big or small? What furniture is there?
> ☐ Now you go into your bedroom. Is it tidy? What furniture is there?
> ☐ You open the window and look out. What can you see from your window?

2 Think about what to say and how to say it. Use the questions in 1 to help you.

3 Tell your partner about your home.

The best in the world

Reading

1 Work with a partner. You are going to read descriptions of three of the best places in the world. Choose the most appropriate description for each photo.

> The best beach   The best palace   The best museum   The best mountain
> The best festival   The best ruin

a Baalbek, Lebanon

2 Match the descriptions (*1–3*) below to the photos (*a–c*) in 1. Do you agree with the selection?

1 It's a perfect mountain, 5,895 metres high. The youngest person to climb to the top was 11 years old and the oldest was 74.

2 This Roman ruin is bigger than the Acropolis in Athens and is nearly 2,000 years old.

3 It was the heart of the Chinese Empire for nearly 500 years. Seven million tourists visit each year.

3 Work with a partner. Talk about the best places in your country. Use the different kinds of places in the box in 1 and your own ideas.

b The Forbidden City, China

Writing

Work with a partner. Student A look at page 88. Student B look at page 100.

c Kilimanjaro, Tanzania

5 *Review 1*

Destinations

> **Language reviewed:** *there is / there are* (Unit 4); prepositions of time (Unit 3); adverbs of frequency (Unit 3); possessive adjectives (Unit 1); object pronouns (Unit 3); *like + -ing* (Unit 3); collocations with *do, go, have, make* (Unit 3)

there is / there are
1 🔈 **30** Look at the photos (*a–c*) and listen to the conversation. Which hotel location are they talking about?

2 Work with a partner. Write a similar conversation about one of the other hotels in 1 or another hotel you know. Include at least one example of each phrase in the box.

> there's a   there are (some)   there aren't any   is there a   are there any

3 Where is your favourite hotel? Describe the location to your partner.

Word stress
1 Look at some of the words from Units 1–4. Say the words and add each one to an appropriate column in the table. <u>Underline</u> the stressed syllable.

> ~~chocolate~~   decision   delicious   different
> evening   interesting   listening   mechanic
> miserable   reception   relation   restaurant
> secretary   vegetable   Wednesday

A	B	C
■ ▪	■ ▪ ▪	▪ ■ ▪
<u>choc</u>olate		

2 🔈 **31** Listen, check and repeat the answers to 1.

in, on, at & adverbs of frequency
1 Complete the following sentences with *in, on,* or *at.*

a) I wear shorts *in* summer.
b) I go dancing ____ the weekend.
c) I have a big party ____ my birthday.
d) I have dinner ____ 8pm.
e) I go to church ____ Sundays.
f) I go skiing ____ February.
g) I watch television ____ the evening.

2 Add words in the box to make the sentences in 1 true for you. Compare your sentences with a partner.

> always   usually   often   sometimes   hardly ever   never

For example: *I sometimes wear shorts in summer.*

Pronouns, possessive adjectives & *like* + *-ing*

1 Complete the table with the correct words.

Subject pronoun	Object pronoun	Possessive adjective
I	*me*	my
you	___	your
he	him	___
she	___	___
it	___	its
we	us	___
they	___	___

2 You're going to read a letter from a homestay family to a foreign student. Use appropriate object and possessive pronouns from 1 to complete the letter.

Dear Roberto,

Welcome to (1) your new homestay. We are (2) ___ family for the next three months.

    There are five of us in (3) ___ family. I'm the boss! (4) ___ name's Janet, and I've got a part-time job in a supermarket and a full-time job at home!

    Ronny is (5) ___ partner. He works for a big multinational company. He loves (6) ___ job, but he works long hours. At weekends we love going to the cinema or watching videos at home.

    We've got three children: Meryl, Meg and Clint. Clint's at college in Barcelona. He says he doesn't like (7) ___ , so we phone (8) ___ every day, but he's always out.

    Meryl's fifteen, and Meg's twelve. Meryl likes listening to loud music in (9) ___ room and writing poetry. Meg's very sweet. Everybody likes (10) ___ .

    We've got a dog called Britney and two cats called Charles and Camilla. We all love (11) ___ .

    We're looking forward to meeting (12) ___ soon.

Best wishes,
Janet, Ronny, Meryl and Meg

3 Imagine a foreign student is coming to stay with you. Write a similar letter introducing your family.

Collocation

1 Combine the verbs in box A with the words in box B to form common collocations.

A	make	do	go	have

B	international phone calls swimming the washing up
	breakfast in bed sailing the ironing a nap after lunch
	for a drink after class difficult decisions dinner for the family

2 Work with a partner. Combine *Do you ever ...?* with the collocations in 1 to make questions. Take it in turns to ask your questions.

For example: *Do you ever make international phone calls?*

The interview

Language reviewed: prepositions of place (Unit 4); questions & short answers (Unit 1); family (Unit 2); present simple – adverbs of frequency (Unit 2); *like + -ing* (Unit 3)

1 📼 **32** You are going to listen to six sentences describing the position of some objects in the picture below. Put a tick (✓) in the box if the sentence is true and a cross (✗) if it's false.

a) clock ☒   c) photos ☐   e) flowers ☐
b) mirror ☐   d) lamp ☐   f) rug ☐

2 Work with a partner. Complete the following tasks.

a) Correct the false sentences in 1.
b) Describe the position of the numbered objects (*1–6*) in the picture.
For example: *1 There's a plant in the corner.*
c) Compare this office with an office you know. What differences are there?

3 Work with a partner. Put the words in the right order to make questions.

a) 's name your What ?   *What's your name?*
b) children got you Have any ?
c) you Do watching football like ?
d) live do Where you ?
e) married you Are ?
f) Why you want do to here work ?

4 📼 **33** Listen and check your answers to 3.

5 Work with a partner. Imagine the questions in 3 are part of a job interview. What do you think is the most suitable order?

6 📼 **34** You are going to listen to and read the sketch on page 25. Compare your answer to 5 with the question order in the sketch. What is the confusion between Mr Fenn and Mrs Kane?

7 Work with a partner. You are going to perform the sketch.

a) Decide who is going to be Mr Fenn and who is going to be Mrs Kane.
b) Practise your parts individually. Think about what voice your character has, what clothes they wear, and how they act.
c) Perform the sketch for the rest of the class.

Why do you want to work here?

Scene An office.

Characters Mr Fenn, a manager
Mrs Kane, a post woman

Mrs Kane knocks on Mr Fenn's office door. Knock,
5 *knock.*

Mr Fenn Yes, come in!

Mrs Kane Are you Mr Fenn?

Mr Fenn Yes, I am.

Mrs Kane Good afternoon, sir. I've got a …

10 **Mr Fenn** (*Talking over her*)
Sit down, sit down.

Mrs Kane Oh, no, thank you, I …

Mr Fenn (*Talking over her*)
What's your name?

15 **Mrs Kane** Um, Sarah Kane.

Mr Fenn Kane, Kane … Is that Kane with a C
or Kane with a K?

Mrs Kane It's K-A-N-E.

Mr Fenn Ah yes, Thomas Kane – I know him.
20 Very nice man – an excellent builder –
is he your father?

Mrs Kane Er, no, he isn't.

Mr Fenn (*Surprised that he's wrong*)
Ah. Is he your uncle?

25 **Mrs Kane** No. We haven't got a Thomas in our
family. My father's name's Albert, and
my uncle's name is John. But listen
Mr, er, Fenn, I just …

Mr Fenn (*Completely ignoring her efforts to*
30 *interrupt*)
Oh. Oh well, never mind. Where do
you live, Ms Kane?

Mrs Kane I live in Luke Street. It's near the
football stadium.

35 **Mr Fenn** Yes, I know. Do you like watching
football, Ms Kane?

Mrs Kane Er no – I never watch football. But
Mr Fenn, I've got a …

Mr Fenn (*Shocked*)
40 You never watch football!!
What do you do on Saturday
afternoons?

Mrs Kane Well, I go shopping or I do the
housework. But …

45 **Mr Fenn** Are you married, Ms Kane?

Mrs Kane Yes, I am.

Mr Fenn And have you got any children?

Mrs Kane Look, I don't know …

Mr Fenn Don't worry, Mrs Kane – we work
50 flexi-hours here.

Mrs Kane I see. Look, Mr Fenn, I've got a …

Mr Fenn Right, where was I? Ah yes, have you
got a job at the moment?

Mrs Kane Yes, I have. I work for FedEx. I'm a
55 courier.

Mr Fenn For FedEx? A courier?
(*Puzzled*)
So why do you want to work here?

Mrs Kane I don't want to work here.

60 **Mr Fenn** You don't want to work here? Well,
why are you wasting my time?

Mrs Kane I just want to give you a letter. Here
you are. Can you sign your name here,
please?

6 Food

Lexis: food

1 Work with a partner. Match the pictures (*a–d*) with the lists (*1–4*) and choose one of the following titles for each list: *Fruit, Carbohydrates, Vegetables, Proteins.*

1 ____	2 ____	3 ____	4 ____
meat	carrots	apples	bread
chicken	beans	bananas	cereals
eggs	peppers	oranges	potatoes
seafood	a cauliflower	a melon	rice
cheese	garlic	a lemon	pasta
		strawberries	

2 Work with a partner. Use the words in the box to complete the lists in 1.

> ~~strawberries~~   fish   cakes   grapes   onions   mushrooms   olive oil
> tomatoes   pears

3 Look at the food in 1 and 2. Write down one item you often eat, one item you sometimes eat, and one item you never or hardly ever eat. Compare your answers with your partner.

Vowel sounds

1 Say the following words from the previous section. In each group (circle) the word with a different vowel sound from the other two.

a) cheese   (bread)   beans

b) pepper   cereal   melon

c) potato   tomato   banana

d) pear   seafood   meat

e) cauliflower   orange   onion

f) apple   garlic   carrot

2 🔊 35 Listen, repeat the words and check your answers to 1.

Food combining

Reading & listening

1 Read the article and complete the sentences.

    a) Don't eat ____ with proteins.

    b) Don't eat ____ with carbohydrates.

    c) Don't eat ____ with any other food.

    d) Eat ____ with any kind of protein or carbohydrate.

2 Work with a partner. According to the rules in the article, which of the following meals will keep you slim?

    a) Steak and chips

    b) Spaghetti bolognese

    c) Fruit salad as a dessert

    d) Fish and vegetables

    e) Fish and rice

3 ▭ 36 Listen to a conversation between Alan and Kathryn about the food combining diet. Check your answers to 2. What is the 'seafood' diet?

4 Work with a partner. Look at page 94.

Eat well, enjoy your food and

KEEP SLIM

Imagine a diet where you can eat three meals a day and forget about calories! With 'food combining', you can eat what you like, but there are some things you can't eat together.

5   'Food combining' is based on clinical research into the way we digest food. The human body digests different food in different ways. Fruit only takes half an hour to digest, but carbohydrates take three to four hours, and proteins take up to eight hours. This is why

10 it is important to eat the same kinds of food together.

    There are many diets based on food combining: for example, the Hay diet and the Montignac method. Some of these diets are complex, but don't worry. You just need to follow a few simple rules and you can

15 eat well, enjoy your food and keep slim.

The three simple rules are:

1 The fruit rule
Don't eat fruit with other food.

2 The protein and carbohydrate rule
Don't eat proteins and carbohydrates at the same meal.

3 The vegetable and salad rule
Eat vegetables or salads with any kind of protein or carbohydrate.

Close up

Nouns: countable/ uncountable

1 Work with a partner. Complete the table with items of food from the photos on page 26.

Nouns you can count		Nouns you can't count
singular countable	**plural countable**	**uncountable**
There's a *melon*.	There are two ____ .	There's some ____ .
There's a ____ .	There are three ____ .	There's some ____ .
There's a ____ .	There are four ____ .	There's some ____ .

2 Work with a partner. Complete the questions and write two possible answers.

    a) *Are* there any mushrooms in picture C?   *Yes, there are.*   *No, there aren't.*

    b) ____ there any cheese in picture A?   *Yes, there is.*   *No, ____ .*

    c) ____ there a cauliflower in picture C?   ____   ____

    d) ____ there any pasta in picture B?   ____   ____

    e) ____ there any bananas in picture A?   ____   ____

    f) ____ there any bread in picture D?   ____   ____

3 ▭ 37 Listen, check and repeat. Work with a partner. Look at the photos on page 26 and answer the questions in 2. Ask and answer more questions about the photos.

Divas

Mariah Carey

P Diddy Jennifer Lopez

Lexis: containers

1 When the famous singers in the photos play a concert, they make a list of demands for their dressing room. Work with a partner. Use words from the box to complete the lists (*A–C*). Then match a list to each singer.

~~vase~~	cartons	bottle
bottles	bars	packet
bowl		

A

- a white room with white furniture
- white candles
- a *vase* of white flowers
- a ____ of Evian water
- vanilla ice-cream
- a ____ of chocolate biscuits

B

- 4 ____ of fruit juice
- 12 ____ of mineral water
- 2 ____ of Cristal champagne
- 2 ____ of white wine
- 20 ____ of soap
- 96 hand towels

C

- pink toilet paper
- 2 ____ of Cristal champagne
- a ____ of fresh fruit
- 12 ____ of Poland spring water
- little trees with lights on
- kittens and puppies to play with

2 🔊 **38** Listen and check. Which singer do you think makes the strangest demands?

3 Work with a partner. Complete these phrases with words from the box.

| ~~a can of~~ | a packet of | a jar of | a tub of | a box of | a tin of |

a) *a can of* coke / beer
b) ____ chocolates / matches
c) ____ ice-cream / popcorn
d) ____ cigarettes / crisps
e) ____ jam / instant coffee
f) ____ caviar / baked beans

4 Work in small groups. Imagine you are a famous singer. Write your own list of dressing room demands. Write exactly how much/many of each item you need.

For example: *I want 54 bottles of pink champagne.*

Close up

Quantity

Language reference p29

1 You use *much* and *many* to talk about quantity. Which word do you use with countable nouns (for example, *tomatoes*)? Which word do you use with uncountable nouns (for example *milk*)?

2 Work with a partner. Complete the following table with the appropriate quantifier.

	●●●●●●	●●●	○
a) How *much* milk have you got?	I've got *a lot*.	I haven't got *much*.	I haven't got *any*.
b) How *many* tomatoes have you got?	I've got *a lot*.	I haven't got *many*.	I haven't got *any*.
c) How ____ cheese have you got?	I've got ____ .	I haven't got ____ .	I haven't got ____ .
d) How ____ peppers have you got?	I've got ____ .	I haven't got ____ .	I haven't got ____ .

3 🔊 **39** Listen, check and repeat. Work with a partner. What is in your fridge at the moment? Ask and answer the questions in 2. Ask three more questions.

4 Work with a partner. Student A look at page 88. Student B look at page 100.

Language reference: nouns & quantity

Countable and uncountable nouns

Nouns you can count		Nouns you can't count
singular countable	**plural countable (add -s, -es, -ies)**	**uncountable**
a melon	two melons	milk NOT ~~one milk~~
a church	three churches	furniture NOT ~~three furnitures~~
a city	four cities	jewellery NOT ~~six jewelleries~~

Note: You can use other words with uncountable nouns to talk about quantity.
For example: a **bottle of** milk; three **pieces of** furniture; six **items of** jewellery

Quantity

With countable nouns you use *How many ...; a lot of ...; not many ...; any ...*
With uncountable nouns you use *How much ...; a lot of ...; not much ...; any ...*

'How many DVDs have you got?' 'I haven't got many DVDs but I've got a lot of videos.'
'How much rice is there?' 'There isn't much rice but there's a lot of pasta. There isn't any bread and there aren't any potatoes.'

Choices

Lexis: *would like*

1 You are going to read and listen to a conversation between a shop assistant (*SA*) and a customer (*C*). Work with a partner. Use the words in the box to complete the conversation. There are three words in each space.

> I   you   would   'd   like

SA: Next!
C: (1) *I'd like* a chicken sandwich, please.
SA: (2) *Would you like* brown or white bread, butter or margarine, mustard or mayonnaise, salt and pepper?
C: (3) ____ ... a chicken sandwich.
SA: Yes, I know (4) ____ a chicken sandwich. But (5) ____ brown bread or white bread, butter ...
C: STOP, STOP. Can you speak more slowly, please?
SA: (6) ____ white or brown bread?
C: Er ... brown bread, please.

SA: (7) ____ butter or margarine?
C: Butter.
SA: (8) ____ mustard or mayonnaise?
C: Mayonnaise.
SA: (9) ____ salt and pepper?
C: No, thank you.
SA: (10) ____ anything to drink?
C: Anything to drink? What is 'anything to drink'?
SA: Coke, orange juice, water ...
C: Ah, drink, drink – coke, orange juice, water. Yes, yes, I understand. ... No.
SA: That's two dollars. ... Next!

2   🔲 **40** Listen and check your answers.

3 Work with a partner. Match the phrases in column A with the situations in column B.

A	B
a) Still or sparkling? / Large or small? / With or without ice?	1 Booking a room in a hotel.
b) Black or white? / Large, medium or small? / With or without sugar?	2 Ordering a glass of water.
c) Red or white? / French or Australian? / Large or small?	3 Buying a train ticket.
d) Single or return? / Smoking or non-smoking? / First or second class?	4 Ordering a glass of wine.
e) Single or double? / Smoking or non-smoking? / Shower or bath?	5 Buying a cup of coffee.

4 Work with a partner. Choose one of the situations from column B in 3.

- Write a conversation like the one in 1. Use phrases from column A in 3.
- Act out your conversation for the rest of the class.

7 Work

Lexis: describing character

1 Work with a partner. Look at the word snake and find ten adjectives to describe character. Use a dictionary. How many of the adjectives are similar to adjectives in your language?

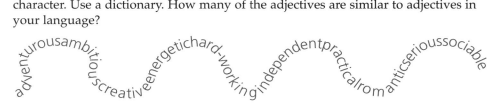

adventurousambitiouscreativeenergetichard-workingindependentpracticalromanticserioussociable

2 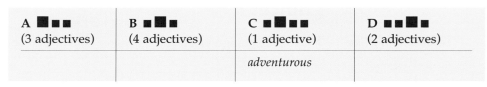 41 Complete the table with the adjectives in 1 according to their stress patterns. Listen, check and repeat your answers.

A ■■■ (3 adjectives)	B ■■■■ (4 adjectives)	C ■■■■ (1 adjective)	D ■■■■ (2 adjectives)
		adventurous	

3 Work with a partner. Student A turn to page 89. Student B turn to page 101.

4 Work with a partner. Follow the instructions to this simple personality test.

- Study the pictures for ten seconds and choose the picture you like most.
- Read the key to your picture on page 94. Compare your results with a partner.
- Read all the descriptions on page 94. Which one is the best one for you?

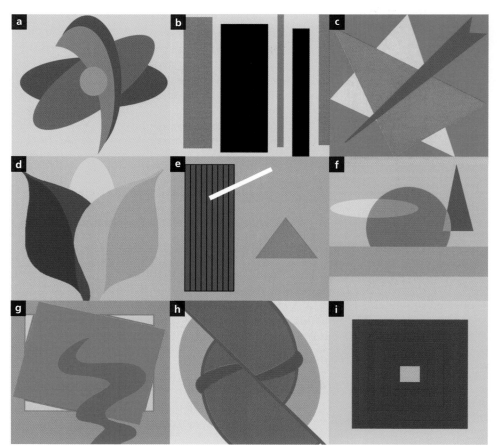

Which job?

Lexis: jobs **1** Work with a partner. Match the characteristics with the jobs. Add one more characteristic necessary for each job.

Characteristics	Job
a) confident, good-looking, slim	1 a snowboarder
b) adventurous, energetic, strong	2 an accountant
c) creative, sensitive, artistic	3 a nurse
d) cheerful, sociable, energetic	4 a model
e) sensible, honest, good at Maths	5 a tourist guide
f) helpful, hard-working, kind	6 a graphic designer

2 Work with a partner, Student A look at page 89. Student B look at page 101.

Reading **1** Work with a partner. You are going to read an article about the model and snowboarder Charlotte Dutton. Which words and phrases in the box do you associate with modeling? Which do you associate with snowboarding?

> muscles   slim   freezing   strong   Paris   warm baggy clothes
> crash helmet   designer clothes

2 Read the article and check your answers to 1.

FROM
MOUNTAINS
to modelling

CHARLOTTE
DUTTON

Born: 1980 **Height:** 1m 72 **Weight:** 51 kg
Hometown: London **Job:** Snowboarder and model

Charlotte Dutton has two jobs. Half the year she's a top model in Europe, and the other half she's a professional snowboarder in Canada. Here she talks about the problems of having two careers.

'I love modelling and snowboarding,' she says, 'but I have to be two
5 different people! You need muscles to be a snowboarder, but you have to be slim to be a model. When I'm modelling I can't eat anything fattening. But in the mountains it's freezing, so you have to eat protein, cakes and chocolate. For the jumps and turns, you have to be strong. Snowboarding is sometimes dangerous,
10 and I often fall. But I have to be careful because I can't break my leg and then go to Paris to model the best skirts. It's funny – half the year I have to wear warm baggy clothes and a
15 crash helmet. Then I go to Europe for a season, and I have to wear beautiful designer clothes.'
    Does she want to be a top
20 international model or an Olympic snowboarder? The answer is she wants to do both ... but when she's much older, she dreams of living in a bakery and
25 eating cakes all day!

3 Imagine you could do two jobs. Which two jobs would you like to do? Discuss your ideas with a partner.

Close up

can, can't, have to, don't have to

Verb structures p115

1 Work with a partner. The beginnings and ends of these sentences are mixed up. Rearrange them to make realistic sentences.

a) A snowboarder *can work from home.*
b) A DJ *has to have very clean hands.*
c) A writer *has to wear a crash helmet.*
d) A tourist guide *can't eat fattening food.*
e) A model *has to know a lot of history.*
f) A cook *doesn't have to get up early in the morning.*

For example: *A snowboarder has to wear a crash helmet.*

2 Work with a partner. Match the <u>underlined</u> part of each sentence (*a–d*) with the correct meaning (*1–4*). Think about your work/school. Which sentences are true for you?

a) <u>I can</u> arrive at any time.
b) <u>I can't</u> smoke.
c) <u>I have to</u> use a computer.
d) <u>I don't have to</u> wear a uniform.

1 It's necessary for me to …
2 It's not okay for me to …
3 It's not necessary for me to …
4 It's okay for me to …

3 Work with a partner. Complete the interviews with *can, can't, have to* or *don't have to.*

Interview A

Interviewer: Cherry Tree, your new film is a big hit. How do you feel?
C: I feel terrible.
I: Sorry?
C: I feel terrible because I hate being famous. It's boring. I (1) ____ go to parties. I (2) ____ sign autographs.
I: But you're …
C: I (3) ____ wear make-up all day. I (4) ____ kiss Brad Pitt.
I: Oh dear. That's terrible. But you're rich now. You (5) ____ buy anything you want.
C: Yes, but there are photographers everywhere. I (6) ____ walk down the street. I (7) ____ go shopping. I (8) ____ go clubbing and I (9) ____ have a private life.
I: Well, why did you make the film?
C: And I (10) ____ answer stupid questions!

Interview B

Interviewer: Max Nova, can you answer a few questions?
M: Sure, no problem.
I: Your film is a big success. How do you feel?
M: I feel fantastic. I love being rich, and I love being famous!
I: Now that you're rich and famous, is your life very different?
M: Oh yeah, very different. I (1) ____ worry about money any more. I (2) ____ buy anything I want. I (3) ____ buy a new car. I (4) ____ buy a big house. I (5) ____ travel first class … and I (6) ____ meet some very interesting people.

4 🔲 42 Listen to the conversations and check your answers to 3. Think of other advantages and disadvantages of being rich and famous. Discuss with a partner.

Language reference: *can, can't, have to, don't have to*

You use *can/can't* to talk about possibility and *have to / don't have to* to talk about necessity.

Possible: *You can smoke.* = It's okay for you to smoke.
Not possible: *She can't eat fattening food.* = It's not okay for her to eat fattening food.

Necessary: *He has to wear a crash helmet.* = It's necessary for him to wear a crash helmet.
Not necessary: *We don't have to do any homework.* = It's not necessary for us to do any homework.

A good job

Anecdote **1** ▭ **43** Think about someone who has a good job. You are going to tell your partner about him or her. Read and listen to the questions. Think about your answers.

☐ What's his or her name?	His/Her name's …
☐ What does he or she do?	He's/She's … (a teacher, a salesperson, a …)
☐ Where does he or she work?	He/She works … (in an office, at home, in …)
☐ Who does he or she work for?	He/She works for … (Fiat, local government, …)
☐ What time does he or she start and finish work?	He/She starts work at … and finishes at …
☐ How much does he or she earn?	He/She earns a (good/average/…) salary.
☐ How much does he or she travel?	He/She … (travels a lot, travels a little, travels …)
☐ Would you like this job?	

2 Think about what to say and how to say it. Use the sentence beginnings to help you.

3 Tell your partner about this person's good job.

Writing **1** Read the letter applying for a job. Five sentences are not necessary – ~~cross them out~~.

2 Where do the following parts of a formal letter go? Match a letter (*a–g*) to a number (*1–7*).

For example: *a) 2*

a) Happy Holidays
300 Railway Lane
Worthing
Sussex

b) Flat 4
65 Green Road
Brighton
Sussex

c) Dear Sir or Madam,

d) Yours faithfully,

e) I look forward to hearing from you.

f) 23rd May 2003

g) *Jason Reeves*

3 Write a letter of application to Happy Holidays for one of the following part-time jobs: sales assistant; waiter/waitress; security guard. Decide on the best application for each job.

(1) ____

(2) ____

(3) ____

(4) ____

I would like to apply for a part-time job as a tour leader with your company during my summer holidays. ~~I don't really want to work, but I need the money~~. I am available from the beginning of June to the end of September.

I am a second-year student at Sussex University. Unfortunately I failed some of my exams this year, but I can take them again in the autumn. I am studying tourism and I think I can learn a lot in your company.

I enjoy working with people and I am interested in learning more about the holiday industry.

I sometimes get up a bit late, but I'm very nice and friendly. I am good at working with people and I enjoy travelling. I can speak French quite well and I can speak a little Spanish.

I can also count from 1 to 10 in German, Japanese, Arabic, Icelandic and Bulgarian.

I am available for an interview any time. I would prefer the afternoon, if you don't mind. You can contact me at the address above, or phone me on my mobile number 09970 340 678.

(5) ____

(6) ____

(7) ____

8 Sea

kite-surfing | scuba-diving | fishing | sailing | windsurfing
rowing | swimming | surfing | canoeing

Work in small groups. Discuss the questions.

- Do you live near the sea, a river or a lake?
- Do you usually go to the beach for your holidays? Where do you go?
- Do you like water sports? Which ones? (Look at the photos above.)

Listening 1 ▭ 44 Three people were interviewed about water sports. The time expressions in the table are wrong. Listen and complete the table with the correct expressions.

LANGUAGE TOOLBOX

Past simple

be	*go*
I was	I went
you were	you went
he was	he went
she was	she went
it was	it went
we were	we went
they were	they went

	went swimming	went sailing	went windsurfing	went scuba-diving
Pete	in ~~2001~~ *August*	–	last week	–
Shanaz	–	6 months ago	–	–
Nacho	on Monday	yesterday	–	last month

2 Re-write the two questions in the correct order and ask your partner.

a) ever you go Do <u>swimming</u>?
b) last was When you the went time <u>swimming</u>?

3 Ask each other different questions by replacing the <u>underlined</u> words in 2 with different sports.

Lexis: time expressions 1 Work with a partner. Complete the table to show two ways of saying the same thing.

	With *on, in, at* and *last*		With *ago*
a)	last week	=	*a* week ago
b)	last weekend	=	____ days ago
c)	in 1998	=	____ years ago
d)	last winter	=	____ months ago
e)	on ____	=	three days ago
f)	last ____	=	eight months ago
g)	at ____	=	three hours ago
h)	in ____	=	ten years ago

2 Write one true sentence about yourself and one false one using the time expressions in 1.

For example: *Last week I went to the cinema. (True.)   In 1998 I went skiing. (False.)*

3 Read your sentences to your partner. Ask him or her to spot the false sentence.

Surfing USA

Reading

1 Read the article about Jack O'Neill, the founder of O'Neill sportswear. What is the meaning of the title of the article (*a, b,* or *c*)?

a) Jack O'Neill never goes outside.
b) Wetsuits keep you warm in cold water.
c) California has a warm climate.

IT'S ALWAYS SUMMER ON THE INSIDE

O'NEILL, the sportswear company, is celebrating its fiftieth birthday. The man who started the company is Jack O'Neill.

As a young man, Jack O'Neill worked for a big company, but he always went to the beach in his free time. He loved surfing, but the Californian ocean was cold. Jack
5 wanted to find a way to stay warm in the water and he started to make protective clothing for cold water, or 'wetsuits'.

At first he used polyvinylchloride (pvc), but then he discovered a better material, neoprene. Neoprene was a material used on the underside of a carpet of a DC-3 plane which O'Neill was travelling on. In 1952 he stopped working for the
10 company and opened the first Surf Shop where he sold surf-boards and wetsuits.

Jack took his wetsuits to all the major boat shows in the fifties. His three young children went with him and sat in a bath of ice, wearing wetsuits. When people asked, 'What's a wetsuit?' Jack pointed to his children.

O'Neill is a family-run company. There are now seven children and they all work
15 for the company. Jack is still chairman and he does a lot of charity work. He looks like a pirate since he lost his eye in a surfing accident.

2 Test your memory! Write down …

a) … where Jack O'Neill went to the beach.
b) … why he started to make wetsuits.
c) … where he discovered a better material for wetsuits.
d) … when he opened his first Surf Shop.
e) … why he took his children to boat shows.
f) … why he looks like a pirate.

3 Read the article again and check your answers to 2. Do you have any clothes by O'Neill? Which other famous sportswear brands do you know? Which brand makes the best clothes? Discuss with your partner.

***-ed* endings**

1 The regular verbs in the box below come from the article. Say the past simple forms and decide if the *-ed* ending adds an extra syllable. Complete the table.

A Same syllables	B Extra syllable
work / worked	*want / wanted*

~~work / worked~~   ~~want / wanted~~   use / used   stop / stopped
start / started   point / pointed   open / opened   love / loved
discover / discovered   ask / asked

2 🔊 45 Listen and check your answers.

Close up

Past simple

Verb structures p114

1 Work with a partner. Look at the verbs in boxes A and B and discuss the questions.

A
enjoy / enjoyed   like / liked
live / lived   stop / stopped
study / studied   travel / travelled
try / tried   watch / watched

B
break / broke   come / came
fall / fell   find / found
lose / lost   put / put   sit / sat
write / wrote

a) Which verbs have irregular past forms?
b) Which verbs have regular past forms?
c) How do you make past forms for regular verbs …
  1 ending in *-e* (*love*)?   3 ending in 1 vowel + 1 consonant (*stop*)?
  2 ending in consonant + *y* (*try*)?   4 ending in any other way?

2 Work with a partner. Write the past forms of these irregular verbs and practise saying them. In each group, ⟨circle⟩ the past form with a different vowel sound from the other two. You can use the *Irregular verbs* list on page 117.

a) go / *went*   do / ⟨*did*⟩   send / *sent*
b) have / ____   sell / ____   tell / ____
c) bring / ____   swim / ____   think / ____
d) meet / ____   let / ____   get / ____
e) read / ____   hear / ____   say / ____
f) can / ____   teach / ____   catch / ____
g) fly / ____   know / ____   buy / ____
h) see / ____   keep / ____   sleep / ____

3 ▭ **46** Listen and check your answers to 2.

4 ▭ **47** You are going to play bingo. Follow the instructions.

- Copy the bingo card and complete it with the past tense forms of nine different verbs in the list.
- Listen to the recording and when you hear a verb on your card, ~~cross it out~~.
- When three verbs in a vertical (↓), horizontal (→) or diagonal (↘) line are crossed out, shout, 'Bingo!'.
- Check your answers with the tapescript on page 122.

become	begin	build	choose	cost	cut	drink	feel	fight	forget
give	grow	hit	learn	lend	make	mean	meet	pay	ring	run
sing	spend	wear	stand	steal	throw	understand	wake	win

5 Work with a partner. Student A look at page 90. Student B look at page 102.

Language reference: past simple

The past simple is used to fix events and situations in the past. You often use it in stories.

*Last year I **went** to Paris. I visited all the tourist sites, ate lots of delicious food and had a wonderful time. It was great!*

Note: Apart from the verb *be*, there is only one past form for each verb – *I / you / he / she / it / we / they* **went** or **visited** or **met**, etc. For verbs with regular past forms add *-ed*, *-d* or *-ied*. For verbs with irregular past forms you have to learn them. There is a list on page 117.

Jaws

1 Read this story about British actor, Richard E Grant's terrifying childhood experience. Are the following sentences true or false?

a) Grant lived in Mozambique.
b) Grant went fishing with his family.
c) There was a dolphin in the water near the boat.
d) Grant fell in the water.
e) Grant's father became a hero.
f) Grant enjoyed the film *Jaws*.

Shark attack!

When he was eight, British actor, Richard E Grant went on holiday to Mozambique with his parents and his younger brother. (1) *One day*, they went fishing in a small motor boat on an enormous lagoon called San Martina. (2) ___ , the motor stopped, and they couldn't start it again. They shouted, but nobody heard them. (3) ___ , something moved in the water near the boat.

(4) ___ , they thought it was a dolphin. But then they realised it was a big, grey shark. It started knocking the boat. The boat rocked from side to side, and they nearly fell into the water. They were terrified. Grant's father tried to push the shark away, and his mother held him and his brother. They thought they were going to die.

(5) ___ , people in a fishing boat heard them and took them home. Everybody in the town heard about their story and talked about it. Grant's father became a local hero. (6) ___ , a local fisherman caught the shark and put it in the main square. Everybody came to see the monster and took pictures of it.

(7) ___ , when Grant saw the film *Jaws*, he relived the terrible experience.

2 🎞 48 Work with a partner. Use the time linkers in the box to complete the story in 1. Listen and check your answers.

> ~~One day~~   At first   After a few hours   Many years later   Eventually
> Suddenly   Two or three weeks later

3 Work with a partner. Look at page 95.

4 Do you have any good or bad stories from trips, journeys or holidays? Make some notes. Use time linkers from 2 and 3 to write the story. Exchange your stories with other people in the class.

Anecdote **1** 🎞 49 You are going to listen to a woman talking about her last summer holiday. Listen and underline the answers she gives.

☐ Where did you go?   a) I went … (to the beach, to the mountains, to Paris, etc.)
☐ When did you go there?   b) I went … (last month, in July, six months ago, etc.)
☐ Who did you go with?   c) I went with … (my family, my mum, my sister and a friend, etc.)
☐ How did you get there?   d) I went … (by bus, by train, by plane and by car, etc.)
☐ Where did you stay?   e) I stayed … (in a hotel, with friends, in a tent, etc.)
☐ How long did you stay?   f) I stayed for … (two weeks, a month, a few days, etc.)
☐ What did you do all day?   g) I … (visited the area, slept, went to the beach, etc.)
☐ What did you do in the evening? h) I … (went out, watched TV, wrote postcards, etc.)

2 Think about your last summer holiday. You are going to tell your partner about it. Read the questions and sentence beginnings in 1 again and think about what to say and how to say it.

3 Tell your partner about your last summer holiday.

9 *Solo*

Lexis: feelings

1 ▭ **50** Listen and practise saying the words in the box. <u>Underline</u> the stressed syllable. Tick (✓) the words you know.

> <u>an</u>gry   bored   embarrassed   excited   frightened   happy   lonely
> nervous   sad   worried

2 Work with a partner. Look at the photographs (*a–f*). Find a word or words in the box in 1 to describe the person's feelings in each photograph. Use your dictionary.

3 Work with a partner. Take it in turns to make the facial expression to go with the words in 1. Guess which feeling is being demonstrated by your partner.

4 How do you feel in the situations described in the box? Discuss with your partner.

How do you feel …

> in an exam?   when you see a baby?   in a traffic jam?
> when you see a spider?   in a fast car?
> when you speak English?   in a club or disco?
> when you sing karaoke?   now?

For example:
A: *How do you feel in an exam?*
B: *Really nervous.*
A: *Me too.*

Solo voyage

Reading

1 Work with a partner. You are going to read an article about a boat race. Read the first part of the report and discuss the following questions.

a) What kind of race did Debra and Andrew enter?
b) How many other teams were in the race?
c) What do you think happened to Andrew?

GOING IT ALONE

Married couple, Debra and Andrew Veal, entered a 3,000-mile rowing race across the Atlantic from Tenerife to Barbados. There were thirty-four other rowing teams.

They started the race together, but Debra finished the journey alone.

2 Turn to page 96 and read the second part of the article. Compare your ideas for 1c with what really happened to Andrew. Why did he leave the boat?

Listening

1 🔲 **51** You are going to listen to a radio programme about heroes. Nelly B answers questions about her hero, Debra Veal. Listen and match the six questions (*a–f*) with the six pictures (*1–6*).

a) How did Debra feel when Andrew left her?   4
b) What was the main danger of being alone on the boat?
c) Did she have any bad experiences?
d) Did she feel lonely?
e) What did she miss the most?
f) Was Andrew there when she arrived in Barbados?

2 <u>Underline</u> the correct preposition in each of these sentences.

a) Debra and Andrew were excited **about** / **with** the race.
b) Debra was always worried **about** / **of** big ships.
c) Debra wasn't angry **of** / **with** her husband.
d) Debra was frightened **of** / **with** sharks.
e) The sharks weren't interested **about** / **in** Debra.
f) Debra was very happy **about** / **with** completing the race.
g) Debra was embarrassed **about** / **in** her husband.
h) Debra was sad **about** / **with** coming last in the race.

3 Listen to the interview again. Tick (✓) the sentences in 2 which we know are true. Do you think the other sentences in 2 are true or false? Discuss with your partner.

LANGUAGE TOOLBOX

Ways of saying *alone*
I prefer to live *alone*.
           by myself.
           on my own.

4 Work in small groups. Debra Veal spent 113 days alone in a small boat. Look at the activities below (*a–l*) and discuss these questions.

• Which activities do you prefer to do alone?
• Which activities do you prefer to do with other people?
• When was the last time you did these activities alone?

a) live   d) study   g) go on holiday   j) go clothes shopping
b) read   e) listen to music h) go to the cinema   k) do exercise
c) drive   f) have lunch   i) watch TV   l) have dinner

Past simple
vowel sounds

1 🔊 **52** Write the past simple forms for the irregular verbs in box A and box B. Then listen, check your answers and practise saying the past simple forms.

A	think: *thought*	know	feel	mean	speak	see

B	fight: *fought*	wake	spend	grow	wear	spell

2 🔊 **53** Match a verb from box A with a verb from box B according to the sound of their past tense forms.

For example: *thought = fought*

Close up

Past simple

Verb structures p114

1 Work with a partner. Complete the questions and write two possible answers.

a) *Was* the weather good yesterday? *Yes, it was.* *No, it wasn't.*
b) *Did* you get up early? *Yes, I did.* *No, I didn't.*
c) *Did* you have a bath? *Yes, I ____* *No, I ____*
d) ____ your mother make breakfast for you? ____ ____
e) ____ you late for work or school? ____ ____
f) ____ your friends call or text you? ____ ____
g) ____ you go out in the evening? ____ ____

2 🔊 **54** Listen, check and repeat. Work with a partner. Ask and answer the questions in 1. Discuss your answers.

3 Work with a partner. You are going to ask your partner questions about past events.

- Complete the questions in box A.
- Choose an event from box B.
- Ask your partner about the event using appropriate questions from box A.

A	**B**
a) What / you / see? *What did you see?*	1 The last film you saw.
b) What / it / be about? *What was it about?*	2 The last foreign country you visited.
c) Where / you / go? ____	
d) Who / you / go with? ____	3 The last party you went to.
e) What / you / do? ____	
f) What / you / eat *or* drink? ____	
g) Where / you / stay? ____	
h) What time / you / leave? ____	
i) How much / you / spend? ____	

4 Work with a partner. Student A turn to page 90. Student B turn to page 102.

Language reference: past simple

You use *did* to make questions and give short answers with all verbs (except *be*) in the past simple.

Yes/No questions	Short answer *Yes*	Short answer *No*
'Did you have a good day yesterday?'	'Yes, I did.'	'No, I didn't (I did not).'
'Did your friends contact you last weekend?'	'Yes, they did.'	'No, they didn't (they did not).'

Wh questions Note: You don't use *did* with *be*.
'Where did you go on holiday last year?' *'I went …'* '**Was** the weather good yesterday?'
'What did you watch on TV last night?' *'I watched …'* '**Where were** you born?'

The life and times of ...

Reading

1 Work with a partner. You are going to read about the life of Greta Garbo. Use the words in brackets to make comprehension questions for the article.

  a) Where she born? (was) *Where was she born?*
  b) When she school? (did / leave) *When did she leave school?*
  c) When she her name to Greta Garbo? (did / change)
  d) How many Academy Award nominations she? (did / get)
  e) How she different from other Hollywood stars? (was)
  f) In which film she the famous line, 'I want to be alone'? (did / say)
  g) When she from cinema? (did / retire)
  h) Where she the rest of her life? (did / spend)

2 Read the article and answer the questions in 1.

I WANT TO BE ALONE

Hollywood legend, Greta Garbo, was one of the most glamorous and mysterious stars of cinema in the 1920s and 30s. She was born in Sweden in
5 1906 and started life as Greta Gustafsson. She left school at the age of fourteen but when she was seventeen she went to theatre school.

She changed her name to Garbo when she moved to Hollywood. She later became an
10 American citizen.

She appeared in twenty-seven films and got four Academy Award nominations. She was not a typical Hollywood star. She kept her private life very private. She never spoke about her love affairs and
15 she didn't sign autographs or give interviews.

She didn't attend her own premieres, and even her own studio didn't have her telephone number. In 1932 in the film *Grand Hotel* she said the famous line, 'I want to be alone'.
20 Many people fell in love with Garbo, and she had several serious relationships. But she never got married, and she didn't have any children.

At the age of thirty-six, Garbo retired from cinema. In 1954 she
25 got a special Academy Award for unforgettable performances, but she didn't attend the ceremony.

She moved to New York, changed her name to Harriet
30 Brown and spent the rest of her life there – alone. She died in 1990 at the age of eighty-four.

3 Who is your favourite Hollywood star? What do you know about his or her life? Tell your partner about him or her.

Writing a biography

1 Here is a summary of Greta Garbo's life. Put the lines in the correct order.

  ( ) a) theatre school at the age of seventeen. She later moved
  ( ) b) in love with her, and she had
  (2) c) school when she was fourteen and then went to
  ( ) d) from film. She moved to New York. She lived alone
  ( ) e) to Hollywood. During her life, many people fell
  (1) f) Greta Garbo grew up in Sweden. She left
  ( ) g) several relationships. But she didn't get
  ( ) h) any children. When she was thirty-six Garbo retired
  ( ) i) in a large apartment until she died in 1990.
  ( ) j) married and she didn't have

2 Think about somebody in your family who was born in the first half of the last century (1900–1950). Write a summary of their life using expressions in the box.

• grew up in (a place)	• fell in love with
• went to (school, college, university, etc.)	• had a relationship with
• left (school, college, university, etc.)	• got (engaged to, married to, divorced from)
• got a job	
• moved to (a new place)	• had children
• lived in (a house, an apartment, etc.)	• retired

3 Compare your summary with a partner.

10 Review 2

Life

> **Language reviewed:** *can, can't have to, don't have to* (Unit 7); quantity (Unit 6); past simple affirmative (Unit 8); past simple questions (Unit 9)

can, can't, have to, don't have to

1 Work with a partner. Test your knowledge of life in Britain. <u>Underline</u> the correct modal in the sentences below.

a) You **<u>don't have to</u>** / **can't** wear a helmet on a bicycle.
b) You **have to** / **can** vote when you are 18.
c) You **don't have to** / **can't** get married until you are 16.
d) You **have to** / **can** buy alcohol when you are 18.
d) You **have to** / **can** drive on the left.
f) You **have to** / **can** leave school when you are 16.

2 Make the sentences in 1 true for your country. Write three other facts about life in your country using *can, can't, have to* or *don't have to*. Compare your sentences with a partner.

Word stress

1 Work with a partner. Say these words from Units 6–9 and <u>underline</u> the stressed syllable. In each group (circle) the word with a different stress pattern from the other two.

a) <u>sen</u>sible   <u>sen</u>sitive   ⟨ad<u>ven</u>turous⟩
b) sociable   independent   serious
c) energetic   romantic   ambitious

d) creative   confident   hard-working
e) banana   margarine   spaghetti
f) cauliflower   potato   tomato

2 🔊 **55** Listen, check and repeat the answers to 1.

Quantity

1 Work with a partner. Complete the questions with *much* or *many*.

a) How *much* money did you spend the last time you went out?
b) How ____ emails did you receive yesterday?
c) How ____ presents did you get on your birthday?
d) How ____ time did you spend studying English at the weekend?
e) How ____ times did you go skiing last year?
f) How ____ fruit did you eat at your last meal?
g) How ____ phone calls did you make yesterday?

2 🔊 **56** Listen and check your answers to 1. Ask your partner the questions.

3 Ask your partner three more questions about the past. Use *How much* or *How many*.

How much was the hamster?
— It cost £200.... ....It came with a personal trainer.

Past simple: affirmative

1 Work with a partner. You are going to read a summary of the life of a famous American. Put the verbs in brackets into the past simple. Who was he?

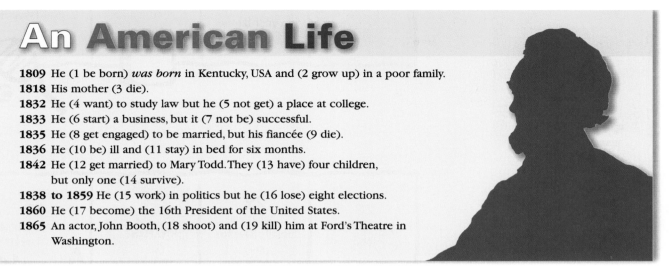

An American Life

1809 He (1 be born) *was born* in Kentucky, USA and (2 grow up) in a poor family.
1818 His mother (3 die).
1832 He (4 want) to study law but he (5 not get) a place at college.
1833 He (6 start) a business, but it (7 not be) successful.
1835 He (8 get engaged) to be married, but his fiancée (9 die).
1836 He (10 be) ill and (11 stay) in bed for six months.
1842 He (12 get married) to Mary Todd. They (13 have) four children, but only one (14 survive).
1838 to 1859 He (15 work) in politics but he (16 lose) eight elections.
1860 He (17 become) the 16th President of the United States.
1865 An actor, John Booth, (18 shoot) and (19 kill) him at Ford's Theatre in Washington.

2 🔲 **57** Listen and check your answers to 1. What facts do you know about the lives of other famous politicians? Discuss with a partner.

Past simple: questions

You are going to try to complete these sentences (a–f) with the names of different people in the class.

- Write a question for each sentence. For example: *Did you go swimming last week?*
- Ask the questions.

a) _____ went swimming last week. *Mario went swimming last week.*
b) _____ made breakfast this morning.
c) _____ slept more than eight hours last night.
d) _____ did the washing up yesterday evening.
e) _____ had fish for lunch yesterday.
f) _____ bought a music CD at the weekend.

Anecdote

1 🔲 **58** You are going to listen to a woman talking about the last time she had a really delicious meal. Read the questions and listen. <u>Underline</u> the answers she gives.

☐ When did you have the meal?   a) I/We had the meal … (<u>last weekend,</u> two weeks ago, etc.)
☐ What was the occasion?   b) It was … (a business dinner, my brother's 18th birthday, etc.)
☐ Where did you have the meal?   c) I/We had the meal … (at home, in an Italian restaurant, etc.)
☐ How many people were there?   d) There were … (fifteen of us, just two of us, etc.)
☐ Who were the people?   e) They were … (my friends and colleagues, our family, etc.)
☐ Who did you sit next to?   f) I sat next to … (Alberto, my grandmother, etc.)
☐ What did you eat?   g) I had … (pizza, steak and chips, etc.)
☐ What did you drink?   h) I had … (some wine, some coke, etc.)
☐ How long did you stay at the table? i) We stayed … (for nearly three hours, all evening, etc.)
☐ Did you have a good time?   j) It was … (great, okay, terrible, etc.)

2 Think about the last time you had a really delicious meal. You are going to tell your partner about it. Read the questions and sentence beginnings in 1 again and think about what to say and how to say it.

3 Tell your partner about the last time you had a really delicious meal.

Let's talk about ...

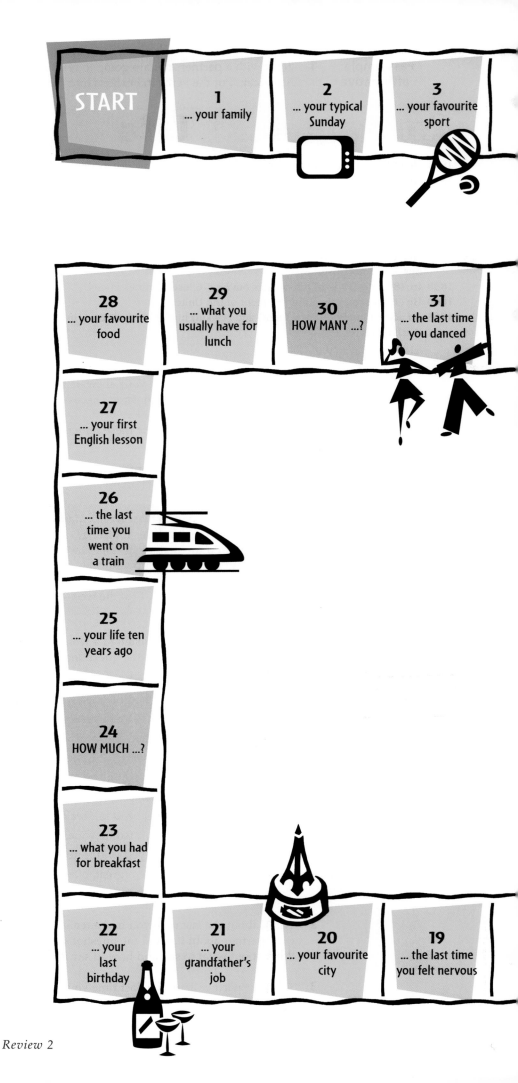

START

1
... your family

2
... your typical Sunday

3
... your favourite sport

28
... your favourite food

29
... what you usually have for lunch

30
HOW MANY ...?

31
... the last time you danced

27
... your first English lesson

26
... the last time you went on a train

25
... your life ten years ago

24
HOW MUCH ...?

23
... what you had for breakfast

22
... your last birthday

21
... your grandfather's job

20
... your favourite city

19
... the last time you felt nervous

4
... food you don't like

5
... one of your relatives

6
WHAT ...?

7
... the last time you stayed in a hotel

8
... a good job

9
... your favourite room

10
... something you love doing

11
... your last holiday

12
WHEN ...?

13
... a good friend

14
... the last time you went to the cinema

15
... your favourite actor

16
... something you hate doing

17
... your house

18
... WHERE ...?

32
... your favourite band or singer

33
... the last time you felt angry

34
... last weekend

35
... your favourite writer

36
WHY ...?

FINISH

HOW TO PLAY

Play the game in small groups. You need a dice and counters.

1 Place your counters on the square marked START and throw the dice.

2 The first player to throw a six starts the game.

3 The first player throws the dice and moves their counter along the board according to the number on the dice.

4 Players than play in turns moving round the board.

5 When a player lands on an orange square they have to talk about the subject for thirty seconds.

6 When a player lands on a purple square, each of the other players asks him or her a question beginning with the question word.

7 If the player has nothing to say or can't talk for the necessary time or can't answer the questions, they are allowed to pass and miss a turn.

8 The game continues until the first player reaches the square marked FINISH.

Looks

Lexis: description

1 Work with a partner. Read the information below and label the photos.

a) Will's got a shaved head. He's got a gold chain.
b) Belen's got wavy brown hair.
c) Simon's got very curly hair.
d) Jem's got spiky hair and blond highlights.
e) Sue's got dark hair and blue eyes.
f) Albert's got short grey hair.
g) Gus's got dark brown eyes and short hair.
h) Carla's got wavy fair hair and brown eyes. She's very pretty.
i) Zainab's got dark medium-length hair. She's got a lovely smile.
j) Nancy's got short curly hair. She's very sweet.

1 ____   2 *Will*   3 ____   4 *Gus*   5 ____

6 *Simon*   7 ____   8 *Jem*   9 ____   10 ____

2 Read the sentences in 1 again. Write words and phrases under the following headings.

Hair length	Hair style	Hair colour	Eyes	Other	Opinion
a shaved head	wavy	brown	blue	a gold chain	very pretty

3 Add more words and phrases from the box to the headings in 2. Which words do you usually use: a) for women and men; b) for women only; c) for men only?

> long   straight   a moustache   green   blond   earrings   glasses   red
> beautiful   a beard   handsome   black   a tattoo   good-looking   a bracelet

4 Work with a partner. Student A look at page 90. Student B look at page 102.

5 Work with a partner. Describe people in the class and guess their identity.

For example:
A: She's got long, straight hair and brown eyes. She's got gold earrings and a bracelet.
B: Luisa.
A: Yes, that's right.

Lexis: *look(s) like*

1 Work with a partner. Match the people on page 46 with the family relations (*a–e*).

    a) a father and his son
    b) a father and his daughter
    c) a mother and her son
    d) a mother and her daughter
    e) a brother and sister

2 Compare your answers to 1 with other students in the class. Use language in the box to justify your ideas.

> I think Jem / Will … looks like Albert.   They've got the same smile / nose …
> They've both got short hair / small ears …

3 🔊 **59** Listen and check your answers to 1.

4 Think about your family. Complete the following sentences so that they are true for you. Compare your sentences with a partner.

    a) I look like ____ because we've got the same ____ and …
    b) I don't look like ____ because we haven't got ____ and …
    c) My father looks like ____ because they've both got ____ and …
    d) My mother looks like ____ because they've got the same ____ and …
    e) ____ look / looks like ____ because …

Lexis: clothes

1 Look at the photograph of Stuart. Tick (✓) the items in the box that you can see.

Clothes and accessories

Footwear
shoes ✓   trainers ✗   boots

Underwear
socks   underpants

Formal clothes
shirts   trousers   jackets
suits   ties   coats

Casual clothes
tops   T-shirts   tracksuits
jeans   sweaters

Accessories
belts   hats   sunglasses
rings

2 🔊 **60** Listen to an interview and <u>underline</u> the correct information. Do you know anyone like Stuart?

    a) He's got **35 / 50 / 350** shirts.
    b) He's got **100 / 200 / 300** suits.
    c) He's got **50 / 115 / 150** pairs of trousers.
    d) He's got **25 / 100 / 125** pairs of shoes.

3 Work with a partner. All the words for clothes in 1 are in the plural form. Copy and complete the following table.

Singular	Plural
a pair of *shoes / trainers* …	2, 3, 4 pairs of *shoes / trainers* …
a *shirt / jacket* …	2, 3, 4 *shirts / jackets* …

4 Work with a partner. Look at people in the classroom. Add clothes to the list in 1 and note down how you count the words: *a XXX* or *a pair of XXX*.

Mr Average

Reading **1**   Which magazines are popular in your country? Discuss with a partner.

2   Read the magazine quiz about the average British man. Do the quiz and discuss the answers with a partner.

IMAGE	QUIZ OF THE MONTH

MR AVERAGE AND HIS CLOTHES

WIN A FABULOUS PRIZE!

1st PRIZE
a weekend for two in the fashion capital of the world, Milan

2nd PRIZE
1,000 euros to spend in the clothes shop of your choice

3rd PRIZE
a free year's subscription to IMAGE

Choose the correct answers below.

How many items of clothing has Mr Average got?

1	a) 32	b) 22	c) 12	pairs of socks
2	a) 16	b) 12	c) 6	pairs of underpants
3	a) 25	b) 20	c) 15	casual tops
4	a) 13	b) 0	c) 8	formal shirts
5	a) 21	b) 7	c) 7	pairs of casual trousers
6	a) 16	b) 6	c) 3	pairs of formal trousers
7	a) 2	b) 4	c) 8	jackets

How much does Mr Average spend?

8	a) 550	b) 350	c) 250	euros a year on clothes
9	a) 140	b) 90	c) 40	euros a year on underwear
10	a) 150	b) 50	c) 15	euros a year on accessories
11	a) 300	b) 200	c) 100	euros a year on footwear
12	a) 1,500	b) 1,000	c) 500	euros a year on cigarettes and beer!!!

Put your answers on a postcard and send them to 'Quiz', IMAGE, PO Box 1480, London W1.

3   Check your answers on page 96.

4   Work with a partner. Refer to the *IMAGE* quiz and discuss the questions.

a)   How many items of clothing do you think Mr Average has got in your country?
b)   Who has got the most clothes in your family?
c)   How many items of clothing have you got (approximately)?

Numbers **1**   ▄▄ **61** Listen and practise saying the numbers.

Numbers p116

> thir<u>teen</u> <u>thir</u>ty   four<u>teen</u> <u>for</u>ty   fif<u>teen</u> <u>fif</u>ty   six<u>teen</u> <u>six</u>ty
> seven<u>teen</u> <u>seven</u>ty   eigh<u>teen</u> <u>eigh</u>ty   nine<u>teen</u> <u>nine</u>ty

2   ▄▄ **62** Listen to four conversations (a–d). <u>Underline</u> the number of accessories each person has got.

a) Hats: <u>14</u> / 40   b) Ties: 19 / 90   c) Rings: 15 / 50   d) T-shirts: 13 / 30

3   Work with a partner. Listen and practice saying the first conversation in 2. Then use different numbers from 1 and practise similar conversations.

Lexis **1**   Work with a partner. <u>Underline</u> the correct verb to complete the sentences.

a)   I always **<u>get dressed</u>** / **get clothed** before I have breakfast.
b)   At the weekend I usually **wear** / **dress** jeans.
c)   I always **take out** / **take off** my shoes before I go into my house.
d)   I never **put on** / **put in** trainers to go to work or school.
e)   I usually **change out** / **change into** casual clothes in the evening.
f)   I always **try up** / **try on** clothes before I buy them.

2   Which sentences in 1 are true for you? Compare your answers with a partner.

The Oscars

Present continuous

I'm talking
you're talking
he's talking
she's talking
it's talking
we're talking
they're talking

1 🔊 **63** Listen to a commentator, Ross White, describing people as they arrive for the Oscars ceremony. There is one mistake in each picture. Listen and note down the mistakes. Compare your answers with a partner.

ⓐ **Penelope Jones**

ⓑ **Melanie Matthews**

ⓒ **Kerry Fisher**

ⓓ **Bobby Finn and partner**

2 Match the verb phrases in column A with the noun phrases in column B. Who is doing each action according to Ross White? Listen again and check your answers.

A	B
a) I'm waiting for	her hand.
b) She's wearing	her car.
c) She's getting out of	her fans.
d) She's waving to	a beautiful blue dress.
e) He's holding	the big stars.

Close up

Present continuous

Verb structures p114

1 Complete these *Yes/No* questions and short answers with a pronoun and the correct form of the verb *be*.

a) *Are* you wearing jeans?   Yes, *I am*. No, *I'm not*.
b) ____ you sitting next to a window?   ____ ____
c) ____ your teacher standing up?   ____ ____
d) ____ the traffic making a noise?   ____ ____
e) ____ the birds singing outside?   ____ ____
f) ____ you having a good time?   ____ ____

2 🔊 **64** Listen, check and repeat. Work with a partner. Ask and answer the questions in 1.

3 Work with a partner. Student A look at page 91. Student B look at page 103.

Language reference: present continuous

You use the present continuous to talk about activities in progress now.

Question	Short answer *Yes*	Short answer *No*
Are you waving?	*Yes, I am.*	*No, I'm not.*
Is it raining?	*Yes, it is.*	*No, it isn't.*
Are the birds singing?	*Yes, they are.*	*No, they're not.*

Compare the meanings of the present continuous and the present simple.

'What are you doing?' 'I'm preparing my lessons.' (in progress now)
'What do you do?' 'I'm a teacher. I work in a school.' (true all the time)

12 Reality

Reading & listening

1 Read this true story about Glenna's experience with dreams and reality. Answer the questions.

a) What kind of list did Glenna write?
b) What kind of pictures did she put in a photo album?

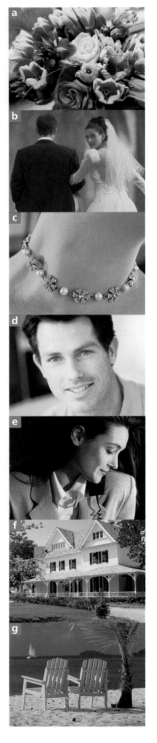

Glenna's dream book

One evening I attended a seminar and heard a man speak. He explained that the mind thinks in pictures, not in words. He said that we can make our dreams become reality. We just have to follow six easy steps.

1 Make a list of things that you want in your life.
2 Imagine pictures of the things that you want in your life.
3 Cut out pictures from magazines of the things on your list.
4 Put your pictures in a photo album.
5 Wait for your dreams to become reality.
6 Remember, there are no impossible dreams.

So I thought about what I wanted in life and I wrote a dream list. After that, I cut up old magazines and arranged pictures of my dream list in a photo album. Then I sat back and waited.

My dream list

1 I want to meet a good-looking man.
2 I'd like to have a traditional wedding.
3 I want to have flowers in my house every day.
4 I'd like to wear diamond jewellery.
5 I'd like to visit an island in the Caribbean.
6 I want to live in a beautiful new house.
7 I want to be successful in my job.

2 Read the story again. Match the things on Glenna's dream list with the pictures *a–g*.

3 🔲 65 You are going to listen to more of Glenna's story. Did Glenna's dreams come true?

4 Work with a partner. Listen again and mark the sentences true or false. Correct the false sentences.

a) She met her future husband in California.
b) She met him at work.
c) He gave her roses every day.
d) His hobby was collecting diamonds.
e) They had a traditional wedding.
f) They went to Hawaii for their honeymoon.
g) They moved into a new house.
h) Glenna told Jim about her dream book before they got married.
i) She left her job.

5 How many things from Glenna's dream list are on your dream list? Compare with a partner.

Reality TV

Lexis: TV programmes

1 📼 **66** You are going to listen to extracts from eight different types of TV programme. Number the types of programme in the order in which you hear them.

1	A game show
☐	A documentary
☐	The news
☐	A soap opera
☐	A sports programme
☐	Reality TV
☐	A chat show
☐	The weather

2 What types of programme do you like/hate? Discuss with a partner.

Writing

1 Work with a partner. Read the online application form below and discuss the questions.

   a) What type of person do they want on *Big Brother*?

   b) How much can you win?

   c) In your opinion, which part of the form is the most difficult to fill in?

Big Brother

Back   Forward   Stop   Refresh   Home   Favorites   History   Search   AutoFill   Larger   Smaller   Print   Mail   Preferences

Address: http://www.bigbrother.com/   Go

BIG BROTHER

DO YOU WANT TO TAKE PART?

- Are you an outgoing, interesting, competitive person?
- Are you ready for anything and everything?
- Are you ready to live inside the *Big Brother* House with eleven other strangers while cameras record you twenty-four hours a day, seven days a week?
- Would you like €500,000?

Answer 'Yes' to these questions and you could be a contestant on *Big Brother*.

Interested? Fill in the form and send it to *Big Brother*, Channel 4, London SW1.

ONLINE CONTESTANT APPLICATION

Title (✓ as appropriate)
Mr ☐   Mrs ☐   Ms ☐   Miss ☐

First name

Surname

Date of birth
Day   Month   Year

Street address

Town / City   Zip/Postal code

Phone number
Day
Evening

Occupation

Hobbies

Five adjectives to describe you

Favourite TV show

Why do you want to be on *Big Brother*? (Be creative!)

Internet zone

Big Brother

A group of adults live together in a house. TV cameras film them twenty-four hours a day. There are versions of *Big Brother* on TV all over the world.

2 Three people gave the following reasons for being on *Big Brother*. Who do you think the programme-makers will choose? Discuss with a partner.

  1 **Eric**: 'I hope to win *Big Brother* and give the money to a friend who needs an expensive operation.'

  2 **Sheryl**: 'I want to go on *Big Brother* because I'm really good-looking. The camera loves me!'

  3 **Lynne**: 'I'd like to meet new people and have new experiences.'

3 Imagine you want to be on *Big Brother*. Fill in the form for yourself.

4 Work as a class. Read each other's application forms. Vote for the best reason for being on *Big Brother*.

Close up

want to, 'd (would)
like to, hope to

Language reference p53

1 Re-write the sentences so that they make sense.

a) I world travel to around want the *I want to travel around the world.*
b) married to I get want don't
c) lots like have of I'd to children
d) be to famous wouldn't I like
e) hope before fifty I I'm retire to

2 Tick (✓) the sentences that are true for you. Compare with a partner.

3 Work in groups of three. Turn to page 96.

(be) going to

Language reference p53

Verb structures p115

1 You are going to read and listen to an interview. Danielle, a TV presenter, is talking to Lynne, the winner of *Big Brother* about her plans for the future. Use the phrases in the box to complete the conversation. You can use the phrases more than once.

> I'm going to   I'm definitely not going to   you're going to   are you going to
> we're going to

D: Lynne, congratulations. How do you feel?
L: Oh, great. I feel fantastic. I'm so happy.
D: What's the first thing (1) *you're going to* do when you get out?
L: (2) _____ have a big party for all my friends. I missed them so much.
D: Ah. What (3) _____ do with the money?
L: Well, (4) _____ give some of it to charity, and with the rest (5) _____ buy a house for my mum.
D: So, which of your *Big Brother* housemates (6) _____ see again?
L: There are some people I'd like to see again, and there are two people (7) _____ see again. I think you know who they are.
D: Yes, of course. That was really horrible. But your hair looks okay now.
L: Yeah, well ...
D: Anyway Lynne, the question everyone wants to ask. You and Eddie became really good – er – friends in the House. So (8) _____ see Eddie again?
L: Well, I don't know. Yes, of course (9) _____ see one another. But we don't know what's going to happen.
D: What advice would you give to future *Big Brother* contestants?
L: Don't do it! No, I'm only joking. Be yourself, and be patient. It's very boring in there.
D: Finally, Lynne, what are your future plans?
L: Well, first (10) _____ go out and spend some money. Then I want to start my singing career. (11) _____ record a CD. Actually, I'd quite like to be a television presenter.
D: Oh – well, good luck.

LANGUAGE TOOLBOX

(be) going to + verb

I'm going to talk
You're going to talk
He's going to talk
She's going to talk
It's going to talk
We're going to talk
They're going to talk

2 🔲 67 Listen and check your answers.

3 Work with a partner. Each of these good intentions has one word missing. Re-write each sentence with the word in the correct place.

a) I'm going do more exercise. (to) *I'm going to do more exercise.*
b) I going to save money. ('m)
c) I'm to spend more time with my family. (going)
d) I'm going book my holidays earlier. (to)
e) I'm going to arrive late for appointments. (not)

4 Which of the good intentions in 3 do you have? Discuss with a partner.

5 Work with a partner. Student A turn to page 91. Student B turn to page 103.

Language reference: future forms

want to, 'd (would) like to, hope to

You use these structures to talk about your dreams or desires for the future.

We **want to** visit India next year.

One day, **I'd like to** climb Mount Fuji in Japan.

My sister **hopes to** continue her studies in the USA.

(be) going to

You use (be) going to to talk about your future plans and intentions.

I'm going to have a big party for all my friends.

We **aren't going to** stay for a long time.

Are you **going to** visit your parents this weekend?

Vowel sounds

1 Say the following words from the unit. In each group (circle) the word with a different vowel sound from the other two.

a) game (dream) wait   c) <u>pe</u>ople <u>rea</u>son <u>is</u>land   e) ad<u>vice</u> be<u>lieve</u> on<u>line</u>

b) mind type drink   d) kind list think   f) week make speak

2 🔲 **68** Listen, repeat the words and check your answers to 1.

3 Say the words in 1 again and add each one to an appropriate column in the table.

/iː/ 6 words	/ɪ/ 3 words	/aɪ/ 6 words	/eɪ/ 3 words
dream			

I Have A Dream

Song

1 🔲 **69** Read and listen to the song. Choose the most appropriate word/phrase to complete the statements below. Compare your ideas with your partner.

a) It's a *positive / sad / romantic / ...* song.

b) I think the song is *great / okay / not bad / ...* .

c) I *often / sometimes / hardly ever / ...* listen to songs like this.

2 Complete these sentences with words from the song.

a) I had a bad d____ last night.

b) I have a particular song that I s____ when I'm happy.

c) I have to c____ with a lot of problems in my job.

d) When I was a child, I had a favourite fairy t____ .

e) I b____ in miracles.

f) I can see s____ good in everyone.

3 Which sentences in 2 are true for you? Compare with a partner.

Abba

From Sweden, Abba were the most popular pop band in the world in the late 1970s and early 1980s.

I have a dream, a song to sing,
To help me cope with anything.
If you see the wonder of a fairy tale
You can take the future even if you fail.
5   I believe in angels,
Something good in everything I see.
I believe in angels
When I know the time is right for me.
I'll cross the stream – I have a dream.

10   I have a dream, a fantasy
To help me through reality.
And my destination makes it worth the while,
Pushing through the darkness still another mile.
I believe in angels,
15   Something good in everything I see.
I believe in angels
When I know the time is right for me.
I'll cross the stream – I have a dream.
20   I'll cross the stream – I have a dream.

13 *Things*

Reading

1 Work with a partner and match pictures *a–j* with the words in the box.

> an address book   glasses   a glove   a handbag   keys   a mobile phone
> money   a pet (snake)   a TV remote   a wedding ring

2 The items in 1 are the top ten things British people are most likely to lose. Which do you think are the top three things? Discuss with a partner. Then turn to page 96 and check your ideas.

3 Work with a partner. Which three things do you think people are least likely to lose? Read the article and check your ideas.

Lost property

The average person in Britain spends a year of their life looking for lost items. Monday is the most common day to lose things.

5   In today's fast-moving society, we have more and more things to lose, more and more places to lose them and less and less time to find them.

10   Research at the University of Central Lancashire shows what men and women do when they lose things. One in five women cry, and more than a quarter of men swear.

15   Some women become violent.

The objects that people are least likely to lose are their car, passport or laptop computer. 95 to 100% of people say they have never lost any

20   of these items.

Of the things people wanted to lose, nearly half said 'boring friends'.

4 Work in small groups. Refer to the *Top ten things* in 2 and discuss the questions.

a) Which things have you got with you now / at home / at work or school?
b) Which things do you often lose / sometimes lose / never lose?
c) When was the last time you lost something? What happened?

Listening

1 70 You are going to listen to a phone conversation between Judy and a Lost property officer. Judy lost a bag yesterday. Which bag did she lose (*a*, *b*, or *c*)?

2 Complete the questions that the Lost property officer asks in 1. Use the words in the box. Listen and check your answers.

> ~~What~~   How   Is there   What kind   Can   What's

a) *What* colour is it?
b) ____ it made of?
c) ____ you give me some more information?
d) ____ big is it?
e) ____ anything in it?
f) ____ of bag is it?

3 Work with a partner. Turn to page 97.

4 Work with a partner. Imagine you lost your own bag. Write a conversation between you and a Lost property officer. Act out your conversation in front of the class.

Shop till you drop

1 Read the article about Karyn. Why did she set up the website *savekaryn.com*?

savekaryn.com

Karyn lives in New York. Six months ago, she had a good job and she earned a good salary. But she didn't save her money. She spent it. In fact,
5 she had a big shopping habit and a credit card debt of $20,000.

There were the Gucci bags, the Prada shoes and the La Prairie skincare products. She had a monthly hairdressing bill, and a personal trainer.
10 She could afford it, but then she lost her job.

She soon found another job, but the salary was much lower ... and she still had a credit card debt of $20,000.

She moved to a smaller flat, bought cheaper
15 clothes and skincare products and went out less ... but she still had a huge credit card debt.

Then she had a brilliant idea. She started a website called *savekaryn.com* and put the following letter on it.

Hello everyone,
Thank you all for visiting my website! My name is Karyn. I'm really nice, and I'm asking for your help! The problem is that I have this huge credit card debt and I need $20,000 to pay it off. All I need is $1 from 20,000 people, or $2 from 10,000 people, or $5 from 4,000 people.
    SO I'M ASKING ...
    Please help me pay off my debt. I am the girl at the office that MAKES YOU SMILE. Give me $1. Give me $5. Hell, give me $20 if you feel like it! I promise that everything you give me will go towards paying off my debt.

And they did. In fact, they sent her $13,323.08 in total, and in just five months she was able to pay off her credit card debt. Now Karyn is an internet celebrity and she is looking forward to helping others.

2 Work with a partner. Discuss the questions.

- What kind of people do you think gave money to Karyn?
- When was the last time somebody gave money to you?
- Who (or what) do you give money to?

Lexis: money **1** Complete each sentence with a word from the article in the previous section.

a) I never *save* money. I always spend everything I earn. (line 4)
b) I _____ too much money last weekend. (line 4)
c) When I go shopping I never pay cash, I always pay by _____ card. (line 6)
d) My mobile phone _____ is always huge. (line 9)
e) I want a new stereo but I can't _____ it. (line 10)

2 Tick (✓) the sentences in 1 that are true for you. Change the other sentences to make them all true for you. Compare your sentences with a partner.

Anecdote **1** ▭ 71 Think about the last time you went shopping. You are going to tell your partner about it. Read and listen to the questions and think about your answers.

☐ Where and when did you go shopping?	I went ...
☐ What did you want to buy?	I wanted to buy ... (some CDs, a jacket, a camera, etc.)
☐ How long did you spend shopping?	I spent ... (two hours, all day, the afternoon, etc.)
☐ Did you get what you wanted?	Yes, I did. / No, I didn't.
☐ How much money did you spend?	I spent ...
☐ How did you pay?	I paid ... (by credit card, by cheque, in cash, etc.)
☐ Did you enjoy your shopping trip?	Yes, I did. / No, I didn't.

2 Think about what to say and how to say it. Use the sentence beginnings to help you.

3 Tell your partner about the last time you went shopping.

The schwa /ə/

1 ◻ **72** Listen and repeat these chants. What do all the vowel sounds in red have in common?

I'm taller than my sister. I'm taller than my brother. I'm taller than my mother. They're not as tall as me!

I'm younger than my teacher. I'm younger than my doctor. I'm younger than my neighbour. They're not as young as me!

2 Are any of the lines in the chants true for you? Use words from the box or your own ideas to make a chant that is true for you. Say your chant to the class.

short / shorter   old / older   fast / faster   slow / slower   rich / richer poor / poorer   quiet / quieter   happy / happier   lucky / luckier

Close up

Comparatives

(Language reference p57)

(Adjectives p115)

1 Work with a partner. The table shows how to form comparative adjectives. Add one more adjective from the box to the appropriate column in the table.

~~rich~~   good   slim   interesting   friendly

+ -er / r	double letter + -er	– y + -ier	irregular	more + adjective
nice → nicer quiet → quieter a) rich → richer	big → bigger hot → hotter b) ____ → ____	curly → curlier lucky → luckier c) ____ → ____	far → further bad → worse d) ____ → ____	generous → more generous sensitive → more sensitive e) ____ → ____ ____

● ● ● ● ● ● ● ● ● ● ● ● ●

Things I'd like

1 I'd like a richer
   boyfriend.

2 I'd like a more
   interesting job.

3 I'd like quieter
   holidays.

2 Work with a partner. Combine comparative adjectives from 1 with nouns in the box – or your own ideas – and think about things you'd like.

a bedroom   a boyfriend   a car   a computer   a father   a girlfriend   hair holidays   a house   a job   a mother   neighbours

• Write two true sentences and one false sentence about things you'd like.
• Exchange your sentences with your partner.
• Guess which of your partner's sentences is false. Discuss your ideas.

3 Work with a partner. Complete the sentences with the correct form of the adjective.

a) I'm *taller* than Alex but I'm not as *tall* as Ben. (tall)
b) I'm ____ than Carole but not as ____ as Denise. (old)
c) I'm ____ than Eddie but not as ____ as Frank. (relaxed)
d) My feet are ____ than Gina's but not as ____ as Heather's. (big)
e) My house is ____ from the school than Ian's but not as ____ as Jake's. (far)
f) My pen was ____ than Kerry's but not as ____ as Lisa's. (expensive)

4 Replace the names in 3 with the names of people in the class to make the sentences true for you. Ask questions to check your information.

Superlatives

(Language reference p57)

(Adjectives p115)

1 Work with a partner. Write the comparative and superlative forms of the adjectives in the box.

~~bad~~   ~~beautiful~~   busy   cheap   famous   far   good   modern   popular   ugly

For example: *bad – worse than – the worst*
            beautiful – more beautiful than – the most beautiful

2 Work with a partner. Student A turn to page 91. Student B turn to page 103.

Language reference: comparatives & superlatives

All one-syllable and some two-syllable adjectives

1 Adjectives ending in a consonant or 'e'.
old – *older than* – the *oldest*
nice – *nicer than* – the *nicest*

2 Adjectives ending in a single vowel followed by a single consonant.
big – *bigger than* – the *biggest*

3 Adjectives ending in 'y'.
happy – *happier than* – the *happiest*

Irregular adjectives
good – *better* than – the *best*
bad – *worse* than – the *worst*
far – *further* than – the *furthest*

Adjectives that have two or more syllables
interesting – *more interesting* than – the *most interesting*
expensive – *more expensive* than – the *most expensive*

Negative comparisons (*not as ... as*)
I'm *not as tall as* my father.

The most valuable things in the world

Reading

1 Work with a partner. You are going to read an article about a dress that belonged to Marilyn Monroe. Guess the answers to the questions. Then read the article to check.

1 How tall was Marilyn Monroe? a) 1 metre 54 b) 1 metre 68 c) 1 metre 82
2 How old was she when she died? a) 36 b) 42 c) 50
3 In what year did she wear the dress at John F Kennedy's birthday celebration? a) 1955 b) 1962 c) 1968
4 How much did she pay for the dress? a) $3,000 b) $7,000 c) $12,000
5 How much did a collector pay for the dress in 1999? a) $765,000 b) $942,000 c) $1,150,000

Happy Birthday, Mr President ...

In May 1962, Marilyn Monroe sang 'Happy Birthday, Mr President' at John F Kennedy's birthday celebration in New York.

5 She wore a skin-tight dress made of silk and covered in 6,000 beads. It cost her $12,000. Her hairdresser said, 'Marilyn was amazingly beautiful that night, like a vision.'

10 37 years later, Christies of New York held a 'Private property of Marilyn Monroe' auction. 1,500 items of Marilyn's property were sold, including the famous dress.

When Christies looked for a model to 15 wear the dress at the auction, they were surprised to find that the 1 metre 68 actress was very slim. 'One of the smallest mannequins we found in the United States was still not the correct size for the Happy 20 Birthday dress,' they said. 'Marilyn was much smaller than people realised.'

When a collector bought the dress for $1,150,000, it became the most expensive dress in the world. The buyer said that it 25 was cheaper than he expected. He was prepared to pay $3,000,000. 'I stole it,' he said.

There are few photos of Marilyn singing 'Happy Birthday, Mr President', but it was 30 her last memorable public performance. She died three months later at the age of 36.

2 What is the most you usually pay for: a) a pair of trainers; b) a pair of jeans; c) a formal dress or pair of trousers; d) a jacket or coat; e) a pair of shoes? Compare your answers with a partner.

Lexis: big numbers

Numbers p116

1 🔲 73 Say the numbers below. Insert *and* into the numbers where you need to. Then listen, check and repeat.

a) 6 6, 1 1 2 *Sixty-six thousand, one hundred _and_ twelve*
b) 1 9 4, 4 5 9 c) 2 5, 0 0 0 d) 1 5 7, 9 4 7 e) 1, 9 1 8, 3 8 7 f) 3 2 4, 1 8 8

2 🔲 74 The numbers in 1 were the highest prices ever in dollars for: *a bikini; a watch; a pair of jeans; a film costume; some pop star clothing; a boxing robe*. Listen and match the items of clothing.

3 What is the most valuable thing that you own. Discuss with a partner.

Energy

Reading

1 You are going to read about Joaquín Cortés, a famous Spanish flamenco dancer. Complete the headings in the article.

> ~~Ancestry~~   Eating   Family   Practice   Shoes   Sleep
> Travel

Joaquín Cortés: *body and soul*

1 *Ancestry*
His long dark hair is a symbol of his gypsy ancestry. He was born in 1969 in Córdoba, southern Spain and moved to Madrid when he was five.

2 ____
He sleeps for five or six hours a night and wakes up full of energy.

3 ____
Cortés practises for more than five hours a day. His dance is so energetic that he loses two kilogrammes during each performance.

4 ____
He has a passion for women, but relationships are difficult because he is married to his work. His family is the most important thing to him – he sees them as often as possible.

5 ____
When he isn't performing, he eats three times a day. But when he is performing, he drinks coffee with milk all day and eats dinner late in the evening.

6 ____
Like a true gypsy, he travels all the time. But his method of transport is not traditional – he travels by plane.

7 ____
Cortés became interested in dance at the age of seven. His uncle, a flamenco dancer, was his hero. At the age of twelve, he was part of a TV ballet troupe, and at fifteen he was a member of Spain's National Ballet company. Now, Cortés buys a new pair of flamenco shoes every month.

2 The beginnings and the ends of these sentences are mixed up. Re-write the sentences so that they are correct according to the article.

a) He sleeps   *as often as possible.* ➔ *He sleeps for five or six hours a night.*
b) He practises   *every month.*
c) He sees his family   *for five or six hours a night.*
d) He eats   *all the time.*
e) He travels   *for more than five hours a day.*
f) He buys new shoes   *three times a day.*

3 Joaquín Cortés dances flamenco. Name five other styles of dance. Which is your favourite style? Discuss with a partner.

/ʌ/ sound

1 Say the following words. In each group (circle) the word with a different vowel sound from the other two.

a) c<u>o</u>me   (h<u>o</u>me)   s<u>o</u>n
b) fr<u>o</u>nt   m<u>o</u>nth   sc<u>o</u>re
c) m<u>o</u>rning   c<u>o</u>lour   st<u>o</u>mach
d) bec<u>o</u>me   <u>o</u>ther   <u>o</u>pen
e) en<u>ou</u>gh   sh<u>ou</u>lder   c<u>ou</u>ple
f) sh<u>ou</u>ldn't   s<u>ou</u>thern   c<u>ou</u>sin

2 🔊 **75** Listen, repeat the words and check your answers to 1.

Once or twice?

Lexis: frequency expressions

1 Put the expressions (A–J) in the box in order of frequency on the line.

> (A) once a month   (B) every ten years   (C) three times a day   (D) every year
> (E) every two weeks   (F) twice a year   (G) once a day   (H) every four months
> (I) twice a week   (J) four times a week

Not very frequent		Very frequent
←		→
B	A	C

2 Work with a partner. Follow the instructions.

- Point to the parts of the body referred to below (*This is my hair. These are my eyes*, etc.)
- Read the questions and write your answers. Use frequency expressions from 1.
- Ask your partner the questions and compare your answers.

My hair:	How often do you go to the hairdressers?
My eyes:	How often do you sleep more than eight hours?
My chest:	How often do you do exercise?
My heart:	How often do you fall in love?
My stomach:	How often do you eat?
My legs:	How often do you go dancing?
My feet:	How often do you go for a long walk?

3 Work with a partner. Student A turn to page 92. Student B turn to page 104.

Lexis: parts of the body

1 Work with a partner. The words in the box are all parts of the body. Put the words into the correct column. Use your dictionary.

> arm   back   finger   chin   ear   foot   hand   head   hip   knee   leg
> lip   neck   nose   shoulder   stomach   thumb   toe   tooth   waist

I've only got one …	I've got two …	I've got …
back	*arms*	*eight fingers*

2 How flexible is your body? Write two things you can do and one thing you can't do with your body. Use the words in 1.

> 1 *I can touch my left knee with my chin.*
> 2 *I can touch my left ear with my left shoulder.*
> 3 *I can't touch my nose with my right foot.*

3 Can your partner do the things you wrote down in 2? Ask your partner to demonstrate.

For example: *Can you touch your left knee with your chin?*

Lexis: collocations

1 Underline the correct collocation for these actions.

- a) Bend your **knees** / **head**.
- b) Cross your **shoulders** / **legs**.
- c) Fold your **feet** / **arms**.
- d) Nod your **legs** / **head**.
- e) Clap your **hands** / **knees**.
- f) Stamp your **legs** / **feet**.
- g) Click your **head** / **fingers**.
- h) Shrug your **shoulders** / **legs**.

2 76 Listen, check your answers to 1 and do the actions. Work with a partner. Tell each other to do some of the actions.

Image

Reading

1 🔲 77 You are going to do a questionnaire. Listen and repeat the words in the box. <u>Underline</u> the stressed syllable. Which three adjectives best describe you? Compare with a partner.

> adventurous charming confident dominant energetic exciting
> impulsive interesting loyal quiet selfish serious shy unfriendly
> unsociable

2 Do the questionnaire and compare the result with the words you chose to describe yourself in 1. Compare with a partner.

HOW DO OTHER PEOPLE *really* SEE YOU?

1 When do you feel best?
a In the morning.
b In the afternoon and early evening.
c Late at night.

2 You usually walk ...
a fast with long steps.
b fast with short steps.
c quite slowly with your head up.
d very slowly.

3 When you talk to people you ...
a stand with your arms folded.
b have one or both hands on your hips.
c have both your hands behind your back.
d touch or push the person you are talking to.
e play with your ear or touch your chin.

4 When you relax you sit with ...
a your knees bent and your legs side by side.
b your legs crossed.
c your legs straight out in front of you.
d one foot under you.

5 Which of these colours do you like the most?
a Red or orange.
b Black.
c Yellow or light blue.
d Green.
e Dark blue or purple.
f White.
g Brown or grey.

6 In bed you lie ...
a on your back.
b on your stomach.
c on your side.
d with your head on one arm.
e with your head under the covers.

HOW TO SCORE

1 a 2   b 4   c 6
2 a 6   b 4   c 3   d 2
3 a 4   b 5   c 3   d 7   e 6
4 a 4   b 6   c 2   d 1
5 a 6   b 7   c 5   d 4   e 3   f 2   g 1
6 a 7   b 6   c 4   d 2   e 1

WHAT YOUR SCORE MEANS

36 or more: People think you're confident, but also selfish and dominant. They admire you but they don't enjoy your company.
21–35: People think you're exciting, impulsive and adventurous. They love being in your company.
16–20: People think you're energetic and charming. You're always interesting.
11–15: People think you're unfriendly, but really you're just shy. You don't make friends easily, but you're very loyal.
10 or less: People think you're serious and unsociable. They think you are quiet and you prefer to spend time alone.

3 Think about a member of your family or a friend for each description in *What your score means* in the questionnaire. Tell your partner about them.

I'm too tired

1 Match the *Top ten excuses for not doing exercise* with the pictures (*a–j*).

1	'I'm too tired.'	6	'The swimming pool is too crowded.'
2	'I've got a headache.'	7	'I've got a cold.'
3	'I've got too much work.'	8	'I haven't got enough time.'
4	'I've got a bad back.'	9	'I haven't got enough money.'
5	'I've got a stomach ache.'	10	'I've got a bad foot.'

2 🔘 **78** Listen to a conversation between Danny and Louise. Tick (✓) the excuses in 1 that Louise uses for not doing things.

3 Work with a partner. Make up conversations like the one in 2. Use your favourite excuses for not doing things.

Close up

Problems & advice **1** Complete these sentences with *too* or *enough*.

a) My life is *too* busy.   d) I'm not relaxed ____ .
b) I've got ____ much work.   e) I haven't got ____ time.
c) I've got ____ many problems. f) I haven't got ____ money.

2 Are any of the sentences true for your partner? Find out.

Verb structures p115

3 Put the words in the correct order to make sentences with *should/shouldn't*.

a) Alex eats too much chocolate. (more He fruit eat should)
b) Bella's computer isn't fast enough. (a buy She one should new)
c) Chris is too stressed at work. (his He job change should)
d) Dana doesn't get enough sleep. (stay She late shouldn't so up)
e) Ed drinks too much coffee. (should He water more drink)

4 Change the names in 3 to make true sentences about people you know.

Language reference: problems & advice

too & enough
You use *too* before adjectives and *too many/much* before nouns.

   adjective   noun   noun
*I'm **too** tired. I've got **too much** work. There are **too many** problems.*

You use *enough* after adjectives and before nouns.

   adjective   noun   noun
*It's not big **enough**. I haven't got **enough** money. Have you got **enough** room?*

should / shouldn't
You can use *should* and *shouldn't* to give advice.
*You **should** get out more. You **shouldn't** work so late.*

15 Review 3

Looking good

Language reviewed: frequency expressions, *How often ...?* (Unit 14); future forms (Unit 12); comparatives & superlatives (Unit 13); physical description (Unit 11)

Frequency expressions, *How often ...?*

1 Work with a partner. Arrange the frequency expressions in the box in the correct order (left to right) from *Not very frequent* to *Very frequent*.

> almost every day   twice a day   every nine days   twice a week
> at least once a week   every year

2 Read this interview with champion long-distance runner, Paula Radcliffe. The <u>underlined</u> frequency expressions are all answers to the interviewer's questions. Write the questions.

For example: *Almost every day. – How often do you eat chocolate?*

PAULA RADCLIFFE

What's life like for one of the UK's most famous female marathon runners? Sam Murphy finds out.

SPECIAL DIET
I have to eat enough calories for my training programme. I eat healthily and I drink about four litres of water a day. But I'm not obsessive – I eat chocolate <u>almost every day</u> and I have a glass of wine from time to time.

TYPICAL TRAINING WEEK
I work for eight days and I run <u>twice a day</u>. I do the hard training in the morning with an easier session in the afternoon. Then <u>every nine days</u> I have a day off.

OTHER EXERCISE
I do a workout at the gym <u>twice a week</u>.

AFTER TRAINING
I sleep for two hours every afternoon and I try to sleep ten hours a night. After training, I take a cold bath or stand in a cold river or the sea for ten minutes. I have a sports massage <u>at least once a week</u>.

HOLIDAYS
I go on holiday <u>every year</u> for three or four weeks and do absolutely no training. I like jet-skiing, lazing on the beach and dancing.

3 Work with a partner. Ask each other the questions you have written in 2.

For example: *'How often do you eat chocolate?' 'Never.'*

Word stress

1 Look at some of the words from Units 11–14. Say the words and add each one to an appropriate column in the table. <u>Underline</u> the stressed syllable.

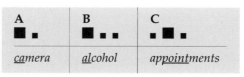

A	B	C
■ ▪	■ ▪ ▪	▪ ■ ▪
camera	*alcohol*	*appointments*

> ~~alcohol~~ ~~appointments~~ ~~camera~~ collector contestant curly dominant
> exercise favourite generous impulsive island jewellery lovely
> neighbour performance selfish stomach successful

2 🔊 79 Listen, check and repeat the answers to 1.

Future forms

1 Work with a partner. Complete the following sentences with *to*.

    a) I want stay in and watch TV this evening.
    b) I'm going buy some new clothes next weekend.
    c) I want get a better mobile phone – mine is very old.
    d) I'd like join a gym and do more exercise.
    e) One day, I hope study at a British university.
    f) I'd like learn another foreign language.

2 Tick (✓) the sentences in 1 that are true for you. Compare with a partner.

3 Complete the sentences below so that they are true for you. Explain your sentences to a partner.

> **Eight ways to improve my life ...**
> 1 I'm going to spend more time with ...
> 2 I'm going to spend less time with ...
> 3 I'm going to eat more ...
> 4 I'm going to eat less ...
> 5 I'm going to learn ...
> 6 I'm going to travel to ...
> 7 I'm going to ...
> 8 I'm not going to ...

Comparatives & superlatives

1 Work in groups of three. Write the comparative and superlative forms for the adjectives in the box.

big   long   good   interesting   far   expensive   old   bad   noisy   safe

My mobile's bigger than yours.

2 Use the comparative forms of the adjectives in 1 or your own ideas to make three sentences about you and your two partners. Use the following sentence frame.

For example: *Eva's mobile phone is older than Paulo's but not as old as Maria's.*

3 Work is small groups. Answer the following questions.

    a) Who is the best-looking man on the planet?
    b) Who is the best-looking woman on the planet?
    c) Who is the greatest film actor of all time?
    d) What is the most exciting sport to do or watch?
    e) What is the most beautiful city in your country.
    f) What is the worst TV programme at the moment?

4 Compare your answers to 3 with other groups. Vote on each of the questions.

Anecdote

1 🔘 80 Think about someone you think is good-looking. It can be someone you know or a famous person. You are going to tell your partner about him or her. Read and listen to the questions and think about your answers.

☐ What's his or her name?	His/Her name's ...
☐ What does he or she do?	He/She's ... (a student, a designer, a model, etc.)
☐ How old is he or she?	He/She's ...
☐ What colour hair has he or she got?	He/She's got ... (blond hair, dark hair, a shaved head, etc.)
☐ What style is it?	It's ... (curly, long, straight, etc.)
☐ What colour eyes has he or she got?	He/She's got ... (big blue eyes, dark brown eyes, etc.)
☐ What other features has he or she got?	He/She's got ... (a lovely smile, a diamond earring, etc.)
☐ What sort of clothes does he or she wear?	He/She usually wears ... (jeans, black tops, suits, etc.)
☐ What do you think he or she is doing now?	He/She's probably ... (studying, watching TV, etc.)

2 Think about what to say and how to say it. Use the sentence beginnings to help you.

3 Tell your partner about this good-looking person.

Clothes

Language reviewed: clothes (Unit 11); present continuous (Unit 11); *too & enough,* *should/shouldn't* (Unit 14)

1 Work with a partner. Look at the scene in a women's clothes shop. How many items of clothing in the box can you see in the picture?

belt boots coat dress earrings jacket jeans ring shirt shoes skirt socks suit sunglasses sweater tie tights trainers trousers T-shirt	

2 Work with a partner. Put the words in the box in 1 in the appropriate column.

I've got a XXX.	I've got a pair of XXX.
belt	*boots*

3 Work with a partner. Look at the different situations and discuss what you wear …

a) on the beach.
b) at a wedding.
c) at work or school.
d) when you go sightseeing.
e) at home at the weekend.
f) at a party.
g) when you do sport.
h) in the countryside.
i) in bed.

4 Work with a partner. The picture in 1 shows a scene from the sketch on page 65. Richard and Ella are in a women's clothes shop. Ella wants to buy a new dress, and the shop assistant is helping. Who do you think says the statements *a–h*? Write *R* for Richard, *E* for Ella and *A* for the shop assistant.

a) I want to buy a new dress.
b) But you've got at least fifty dresses.
c) Can I help you?
d) I'm just looking.
e) Can I try on this dress, please?
f) The changing room is over there.
g) Have you got a bigger size?
h) It suits you, madam. It's perfect.

5 ▭ 81 Listen and read the sketch on page 65. Check your answers to 4. Why does Richard say 'OH NOOOOO!' at the end?

6 Work in groups of three. You are going to perform the sketch.

a) Decide who is going to be Richard, who is going to be Ella, and who is going to be the shop assistant.
b) Practise your parts individually. Think about what voice your character has, what clothes they wear, and how they act.
c) Perform the sketch for the rest of the class.

I haven't got anything to wear

Scene	A woman's clothes shop
Characters	Ella, Richard's wife
	Richard, Ella's husband
	Shop assistant

5 *Richard and Ella are on the street, outside a woman's clothes shop.*

Richard	*(Tired and unhappy)*
	Where are we going now?
Ella	I want to buy a new dress for Betty's
10	party.
Richard	But you've got at least fifty dresses.
Ella	Fifty?! Don't be silly. I haven't got
	anything to wear. Come on.

The shop door opens – music. Richard and Ella
15 *go in.*

Assistant	Can I help you?
Ella	No, thank you, I'm just looking.
Assistant	Are you looking for daytime or evening?
Ella	Evening. I'm going to a party.
20 **Assistant**	The evening dresses are over there.
Ella	Okay, thanks ... Hey, look at this dress,
	Richard. Do you like it?
Richard	*(Trying to show interest)*
	Yes, yes. It's, um, it's a nice, er, colour.
25 **Ella**	Excuse me. Can I try on this dress,
	please?
Assistant	Certainly. The changing room's over
	there.
Ella	Come on, Richard.
30 **Richard**	Yes, I'm here.

Musical interlude.

Ella	What do you think, Richard?
Richard	*(Too quickly)*
	Yes, it's very nice. You should buy it.
35 **Ella**	I don't know. I think it's too small. Have
	you got a bigger size?

Assistant	Not in that colour. But I've got a bigger
	size in red.
Ella	Red? I don't know. What do you think,
40	Richard?
Richard	Eh, what?
Ella	A red dress.
Richard	Yes, lovely. I like red.
Ella	Can I try it on?
45 **Richard**	*(Groans)*
	Oh no. I'm missing the football.
Ella	Richard, this is important.
Assistant	Here you are, madam.
Ella	Thank you.

50 *Musical interlude.*

Ella	What do you think?
Assistant	It suits you, madam. It's perfect.
Ella	Richard?
Richard	*(Trying harder to show interest)*
55	Yes, I love it. It's lovely. You look like a
	film star.
Ella	Do you think it's big enough? Isn't my
	stomach too fat?
Richard	Fat? What are you talking about?
60 **Ella**	So you really like it?
Richard	*(Impatient)*
	Yes.
Ella	Okay, I'll take it.
Richard	Good. Can we go home now?
65 **Ella**	Well, I just want to get a pair of shoes.
Richard	Shoes?? You've got at least a thousand
	pairs of shoes.
Ella	Don't be silly. Come on ...
Richard	OH NOOOOO!

16 *dotcom*

Lexis: *to*-infinitives

1 Work with a partner. Match each website address with a reason for using it.

Click here ...

a)	www.cheapflights.com	1	to buy books.
b)	www.yahoo.com	2	to buy and sell things.
c)	www.flowers2send.com	3	to buy plane tickets.
d)	www.eBay.com	4	to order flowers.
e)	www.amazon.com	5	to get information about parties.
f)	www.world-party.com	6	to search for information on the internet.

2 Which of the websites in 1 do you know or use? What other websites do you use? Why do you use them? Discuss with a partner.

For example: *I use www.cheapflights.com to find out flight times and to buy plane tickets.*

3 Why do you use the following things? Choose two sentence beginnings and complete them in as many ways as you can. Compare your sentences with a partner.

a) I use my computer to _____ .
b) I use my mobile phone to _____ .
c) I use my car to _____ .
d) I use my credit card to _____ .
e) I use my personal organiser to _____ .
f) I use my English to _____ .

For example: *I use my computer to send and receive emails, to find information ... etc.*

Lexis: computer terms

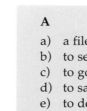

1 ▭ **82** Listen to the first conversation between Tom and his mum. What does Tom's mum want to do?

2 Listen again and tick (✓) the computer terms which Tom's mum understands. Put a cross (✗) by the terms she doesn't understand.

a) surf the net ✓
b) send an email
c) icon
d) desktop
e) click
f) mouse

3 ▭ **83** Listen to the second conversation. <u>Underline</u> the computer terms in column A that Tom uses.

	A		B
a)	a file	1	to move information from the internet to your computer.
b)	to search	2	to use your computer to look for information on the internet.
c)	to go online	3	a flat surface on a computer where you see words and pictures.
d)	to save	4	to access a website, for example by typing in a password.
e)	to download	5	a row of icons on a computer screen that perform actions when you click on them.
f)	a screen	6	to remove something from a computer.
g)	to delete	7	to connect to the internet.
h)	a toolbar	8	a set of information such as a document or a picture that is stored on your computer.
i)	to log on	9	to make your computer retain information that you have put into it.

4 Work with a partner. Match the terms in column A in 3 with the definitions in column B. For example: *a) – 8.*

5 Work in small groups. Write more English computer terms that are used in your language(s). Compare your lists. Which group has the longest list?

dotcom success

Reading **1** You're going to read an article about one of the most successful websites in Britain. Read the article quickly and discuss these questions with a partner.

a) What can you do if you log on to www.friendsreunited.com?
b) Why is www.friendsreunited.com so successful in Britain?
c) Do similar websites exist in your country?

Where are they now?

www.friendsreunited.com is one of the most visited websites in Britain. Nearly ten million people log on to the site every day to find out what old friends are doing now.

5 Julie and Steve Pankhurst are the husband and wife team behind Friends Reunited. They met when they were both software engineers in the same company.

Julie had the original idea for the site in July 1999
10 when she was pregnant with her first child. She gave up her job and set up the website as a hobby.

Friends Reunited now has millions of registered members. The company has spent nothing on advertising – they don't need the publicity because
15 everybody's talking about it. Word of mouth is their best advert.

'Whilst the British are generally quite reserved,' says Steve. 'Everyone wants to know what old classmates are doing.'

20 The couple and their business partner have taken on twelve staff who work from home. Most of them are mothers who Julie met in hospital when she had her baby. Julie's sister works for the company, and a neighbour answers the emails.

25 The site has had many success stories – one man has been reunited with his mother after 53 years. Another was recently reunited with his cat after ten years. (His friend from university
30 had looked after it.) Many childhood sweethearts have been reunited and are now back together, some engaged
35 to be married. The oldest member is a 99-year-old woman who is looking for old school
40 friends.

2 Read the article more carefully and mark the sentences true or false. Correct the false sentences.

a) The person who had the original idea for the website was a pregnant woman.
b) His/Her previous job was as an accountant.
c) The website is advertised on television.
d) The website is popular because it helps people find old friends.
e) The offices are in a university.
f) The company employs 1,200 people.

3 How many old school friends do you still see now? Think about your primary school, your secondary school and your university. Compare with your partner.

Lexis: phrasal verbs **1** Complete the phrasal verbs in the sentences with the correct particle (*after, on, out, up*).

a) I log *on* to the internet at least once a day. (line 3)
b) I'd like to find ____ what my old classmates are doing now. (line 3)
c) I'm not going to give ____ my job when I have a baby. (line 11)
d) I want to set ____ a website one day. (line 11)
e) I'd never take ____ family members in my own business. (line 21)
f) I sometimes look ____ my neighbour's pet when they go on holiday. (line 30)

2 Match the meaning of each phrasal verb in 1 with a word or expression in the box.

> create   be responsible for   access   employ   stop   discover

3 Are any of the statements in 1 true for you? Compare with a partner.

Reading Work with a partner. Student A turn to page 92. Student B turn to page 104.

Close up

Past participles

Irregular verbs p117

1 Copy and complete the verb table with the three forms for each verb in the box. Which verbs have irregular forms?

change do go hear make meet record spend travel visit

Infinitive	Past simple	Past participle
change	*changed*	*changed*

2 🔊 84 Darren and Geoff meet up after getting back in touch through the Friends Reunited website. Use each past participle from 1 to complete their conversation. Listen, read and check your answers.

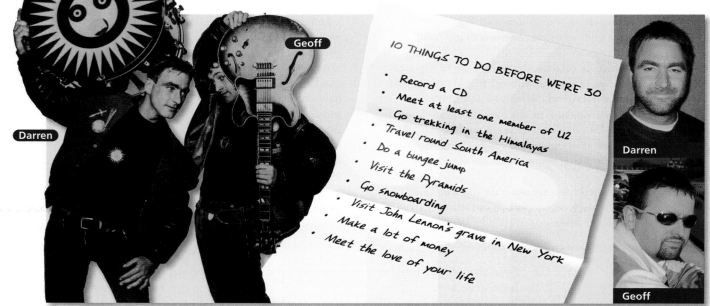

Geoff

Darren

Darren

Geoff

10 THINGS TO DO BEFORE WE'RE 30
- Record a CD
- Meet at least one member of U2
- Go trekking in the Himalayas
- Travel round South America
- Do a bungee jump
- Visit the Pyramids
- Go snowboarding
- Visit John Lennon's grave in New York
- Make a lot of money
- Meet the love of your life

D: Geoff?

G: Darren! Wow, you haven't (1) *changed* at all.

D: And you look exactly the same – good to see you.

G: Wow, I can't believe it – after fifteen years.

D: Yeah. Have you (2) _____ from any other old classmates?

G: Yes, a couple of people – that Friends Reunited website is brilliant.

D: Hey, have you got that list?

G: Yes, here it is.

D: Oh yes, I remember. '10 things to do before we're 30'. Well, we're 29 – how many things have *you* (3) _____?

G: Not many – three, I think. I've been snowboarding, and I've done a bungee jump, and I've (4) _____ John Lennon's grave in New York. And that's it, really. What about you?

D: Let's see – I haven't (5) _____ a CD – I stopped playing music when I left school.

G: Yeah, me too.

D: And I've been to a U2 concert but I haven't met them.

G: Have you (6) _____ much?

D: Well, I've (7) _____ to South America three times.

G: Wow.

D: But I haven't been to the Himalayas yet, or Egypt.

G: Have you ever been snowboarding?

D: Yes, I've done that. But I haven't done a bungee jump. I haven't (8) _____ a lot of money either – I'm a teacher!

G: Ha ha. I've made a lot of money, but I've (9) _____ it. Anyway, have you met the love of your life?

D: No, I haven't (10) _____ anyone special yet. How about you?

G: Yes, I forgot to tell you. I'm married to Pamela.

D: Pamela?

G: Yes, you know, the gorgeous singer in our band.

3 Work with a partner. Refer to the list '10 things to do before we're 30' and discuss.

a) Which things has Geoff done?

b) Which things has Darren done?

c) Which things have you done?

Present perfect

Verb structures p114

'You haven't changed a bit.'

1 Work with a partner. Complete the questions and write two possible answers.

a) *Have* you ever visited the website for your old school?   *Yes, I have.*   *No, I haven't.*
b) *Has* your school ever tried to get in touch with you?   *Yes, it ____ .   No, it ____ .*
c) ____ you ever been to a reunion at your school?   ____   ____
d) ____ you ever received an email from an old friend?   ____   ____
e) ____ your parents ever sent you an email?   ____   ____
f) ____ you ever met somebody new on the internet?   ____   ____

2 ▭ 85 Listen, check and repeat. Work with a partner. Ask and answer the questions in 1. Discuss your answers.

3 The questions and answers in 1 refer to completed actions in 'time up to now'. What is the name of the tense used? How do you form the affirmative, negative and question forms of this tense?

4 Work with a partner. Student A turn to page 93. Student B turn to page 105.

Language reference: present perfect

You can use the present perfect to describe completed actions that have taken place in 'time up to now'.
You often use *ever* to mean 'in your life'.

'*Have* you **ever met** somebody on the internet?' 'Yes, I have. / No, I haven't.'

'*Has* your teacher **ever spoken** to you in your own language?' 'Yes, he has. / No, he hasn't.'

Note: You cannot use the present perfect if you want to describe *when* a completed action took place. You must use the past simple.

I went to Paris three years ago.
NOT ~~I've been to Paris three years ago.~~

He met the love of his life in 1996.
NOT ~~He's met the love of his life in 1996.~~

'Time up to now'

The past				Now

↑   ↑   ↑   ↑   ↑

I've been to Paris many times.

Anecdote

1 ▭ 86 Think about an old school friend you would like to get in touch with. You are going to tell your partner about him or her. Read and listen to the questions and think about your answers.

☐ What's his or her name?
☐ Where did you first meet?
☐ How old were you?
☐ Why did you become friends?
☐ What sort of things did you talk about?
☐ What sort of things did you do together?
☐ What is your best memory of him or her?
☐ When was the last time you saw him or her?
☐ What do you think he or she is doing now?
☐ Why would you like to get in touch with him or her?

His/Her name's ...
We first met ... (at school, at a sports club, etc.)
I ... (was 17, can't remember, etc.)
Because ... (we liked the same music, etc.)
We talked about ... (boyfriends, girlfriends, etc.)
We ... (went shopping, went out, etc.)
My best memory is ... (our holiday in ..., etc.)
The last time I saw him/her was ... (in 1997, etc.)
I think ... (he/she's living abroad, etc.)
I'd like to get in touch because ... (I always liked him/her, he/she had a great sense of humour, etc.)

2 Think about what to say and how to say it. Use the sentence beginnings to help you.

3 Tell your partner about this old school friend.

17 Drive

Reading

1 Work with a partner. You are going to read an article about the best and the worst drives to work. Read these sentences. Put *B* if you think it refers to the best drive and *W* if you think it refers to the worst drive.

a) Jack believes that his drive to work is the most spectacular drive in the world. *B*
b) Her office is seven kilometres from her house, but it takes two hours to get there.
c) Every morning, he drives to work along the coast.
d) Traffic moves down Sukhumvit Road in the centre at half a kilometre an hour.
e) 'Now, everybody has a car, and there aren't enough roads in the city.'
f) As he drives through the National Park, he often sees koalas.

2 Read the article and check your answers. Which drive is similar to your drive to work/school? Tell your partner.

Driving to work

THE BEST DRIVE

JACK SPENCER has an unusual job. He's a lighthouse tour guide. Cape Otway lighthouse is situated near the Great Ocean Road, about 200 kilometres from Melbourne in southern Australia.

Jack believes that his drive to work is the most spectacular drive in the world.

'Hundreds of thousands of tourists come to Victoria every year to drive along the Great Ocean Road and see the amazing scenery. I do it every day on my way to work,' he says. Jack lives in Portland, about fifty kilometres from Cape Otway.

Every morning, he drives to work along the coast. It takes him about forty minutes. 'Traffic isn't a problem,' Jack says. 'I'm usually on the road before the tourists get up.'

He drives past dramatic rock formations like The Twelve Apostles, through rainforest and past spectacular waterfalls. As he drives through the National Park, he often sees koalas. 'From the top of my lighthouse, I have the best view in the world.' says Jack.

THE WORST DRIVE

SIRIWAN lives in the Thai capital, Bangkok, with her husband and two children.

Her office is seven kilometres from her house, but it takes her two hours to get there by car in the morning.

'Some cities have problems with crime, taxes, bad weather – here we have traffic jams,' says Siriwan.

Before she goes to the office, she has to take her children to school – so she sets off from her house at 5 am. The children sleep until they arrive at school. Then Siriwan wakes them up, and gives them breakfast in the car. The children go into school, and Siriwan begins her journey to the office.

In the evening, the traffic is even worse. Traffic moves down Sukhumvit Road in the centre at half a kilometre an hour. In the rainy season it doesn't move at all.

But why is it so bad? 'In the past more people moved around Bangkok by boat. Now, everybody has a car, and there aren't enough roads in the city. The new skytrain has helped a bit, but at the moment it only has two lines.'

Close up

Questions with
***How* + adverb/adjective**
& *What* + noun

1 Work with a partner. Complete the comprehension questions for the article on page 70 with words from the box.

> ~~far~~   far   fast   long   long   many   often   sort   time

a) How *far* is it from Cape Otway to Melbourne?
b) How _____ tourists come to Victoria every year?
c) How _____ does Jack drive along the Great Ocean Road?
d) How _____ does it take Jack to drive to work?
e) What _____ of scenery does Jack drive through?
f) How _____ is it from Siriwan's house to her office?
g) How _____ does it take Siriwan to get to her office?
h) What _____ does Siriwan set off from her house?
i) How _____ does the traffic move down Sukhumvit Road in the evening?

2 Read the article on page 70 again and answer the questions in 1.

3 Work with a partner. Student A turn to page 93. Student B turn to page 105.

Language reference: question forms

Questions with *How* + adverb/adjective & *What* + noun

You can form many different questions by combining *How* + adjective/adverb (*How ...
far, many, often, tall*, etc.) and *What* + noun (*What ... colour, size, sort, time*, etc.).

question words	(auxiliary) verb	subject	
What time	*do*	*you*	*get up?*
How many people	*can*	*you*	*get in your car?*
How long	*does*	*it*	*take you to get to work?*

Lexis: prepositions
of movement

LANGUAGE TOOLBOX

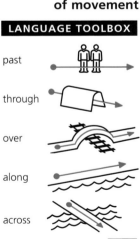

past

through

over

along

across

up

down

into

out of

1 Work with a partner. Choose the correct alternative to complete these sentences.

On my way to work ...

a) I go **down / through** the stairs.
b) I go **out of / along** my apartment.
c) I go **through / across** the street.
d) I go **through / along** the park.
e) I go **into / along** the river.
f) I go **up / over** a bridge.
g) I go **across / up** a hill.
h) I go **past / down** some shops.
i) I go **into / down** my office.

2 Think about your own way to work or school. How many of the sentences in 1 are true for you? Compare with a partner.

3 Write a description of your way to work or school. Try to use all the prepositions in 1 at least once. Re-order the sentences and change the underlined words as necessary. Compare your description with a partner's.

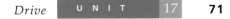

It drives me mad!

Listening **1** ▣ 87 You are going to listen to six people talking about what drives them mad on the road. Listen and match the people (*1–6*) to the pictures (*a–f*).

2 Work with a partner. Complete the following task.

- Match key words and expressions in the box with the pictures in 1.
  For example: *a) – indicate …*
- Think of three situations that drive you mad on the road. Use the situations in 1 or your own ideas.
- Tell your partner. Begin: *'I can't stand it when …'*

> impossible to overtake   park on the pavement   pedestrians   ~~indicate~~
> turn left   turn right   go straight on   get stuck in traffic jams   rush hour
> road works   go on the motorway   have an accident   the traffic lights

Ordinal numbers **1** ▣ 88 Work with a partner. Complete the following table. Listen and repeat the ordinal numbers.

1st	2nd	3rd	4th		6th	7th		9th	
first				*fifth*		*eighth*			*tenth*

2 ▣ 89 Look at the street plan. Listen to three sets of directions from A to B. Match starting points A1, A2, A3 with finishing points B1, B2, B3.

1 A1 → ____
2 A2 → ____
3 A3 → ____

3 Work with a partner. Use the map and take it in turns to give directions from A to B. Then think about the area around your school. Take it in turns to give similar directions to shops, bars, restaurants, etc. near the school.

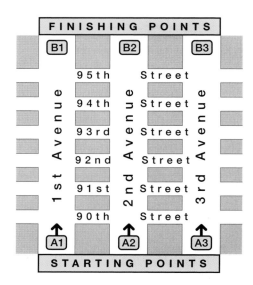

On the way home

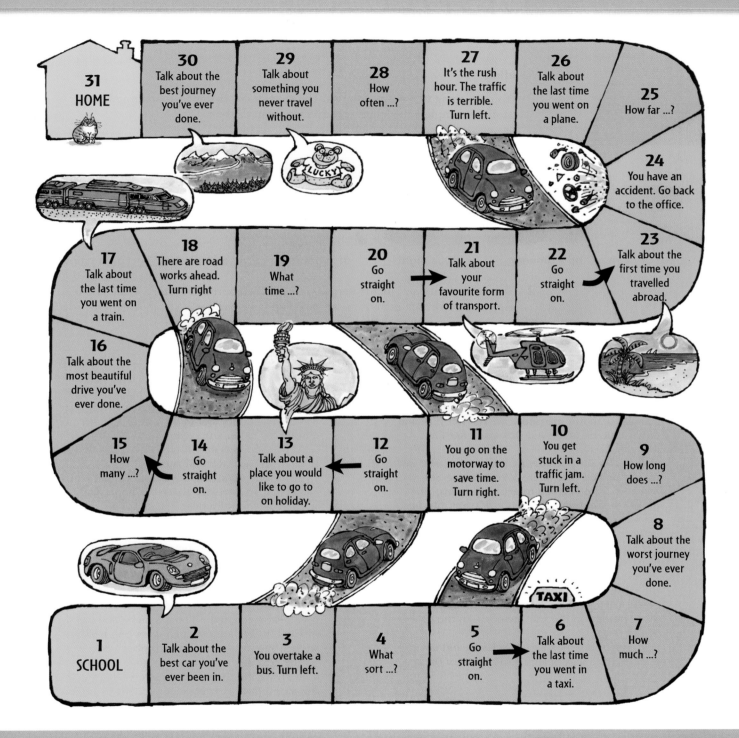

HOW TO PLAY

Play the game in small groups. You will need a dice and counters.

1 Place your counters on the square marked SCHOOL and throw the dice.

2 The first player to throw a six starts the game.

3 The first player throws the dice and moves their counter along the road according to the number on the dice.

4 Players then play in turns moving along the road.

5 When a player lands on a green square they have to talk about the subject for 30 seconds.

6 When a player lands on a blue square, each of the other players asks him or her a question beginning with the question words. If a player has nothing to say, they are allowed to pass and miss a turn.

7 When a player lands on a red square they have to follow the instructions.

8 The game continues until the first player reaches the square marked HOME.

18 Justice

Reading

1 You are going to read two stories. The six pictures below (*a–f*) are important in the stories. Complete the labels with the words in the box.

> ~~paint~~   bag   wine   club   scissors   party

a) a pot of *paint*   b) a dinner ____   c) a night ____   d) a bottle of ____   e) a plastic ____   f) a pair of ____

2 Read the stories and match items *a–f* in 1 to the appropriate story. What is the importance of each item in the stories? Tell your partner.

Revenge is sweet

When Lady Sally Moon found out that her husband was having an affair, she didn't leave him. She thought it was better to be unhappily married than not married at all. But her husband
5 didn't hide his affair, and this made her feel really bad.

One day she was driving home when she saw his car parked outside his lover's house. She was angry and she decided to get her revenge. She
10 quickly drove home, put a pot of paint into her car and drove to the lover's house.

Then she poured thick white paint all over her husband's beautiful new black car.

Next, she carefully took his collection of fine
15 wines from the cellar. That night she went round the village where she lived, and quietly placed a bottle of wine on each doorstep. She left the other bottles on the war memorial in the centre of the village.
20 Finally, she took a pair of scissors and cut off the arms and legs of all his suits – 38 of them in all.

Dinner by post

Last year, I went out with Hermione for four months. We were very different. I always arrived early; she always arrived late. I was very tidy; she was terribly untidy. But to be honest, I found the
5 differences rather attractive.

At first, she was only fifteen or twenty minutes late. But she got later and later.

At the end of August, it was my birthday. I'm a good cook, so I decided to have a dinner party
10 and I invited four friends.

That evening, my four friends arrived on time, but unsurprisingly Hermione wasn't there at eight o'clock. But then she wasn't there at nine o'clock, half past nine or ten o'clock.
15 This was extremely late, even for Hermione. So I phoned her mobile. When she answered, music was playing loudly in the background. 'Where are you?' I shouted angrily. 'I'm at a night club,' she shouted back. I was furious. I went into the
20 kitchen and put her meal into a plastic bag.

The next morning I posted it to her with a note saying, 'Here's your dinner.' A week later I got a postcard from Hermione. It said, 'Too much salt.'

3 ▭ 90 Work with a partner. Choose a suitable ending for each story. Read and listen and check your answers.

a) The following week, I had another dinner party.
b) As you can imagine, I never saw her again.
c) Her husband wasn't very happy when he got home.
d) In the end, I apologised to my friends.
e) After that, she felt much better.
f) A few days later, she went skiing.

4 Which story do you like best? Tell your partner why.

Lexis: time adverbials

1 Read the stories on page 74 again. Write the time adverbials in the box in the order in which they appear in the stories.

> ~~One day~~   ~~Last year~~   At first   Then   At the end of August   Next
> That night   That evening   The next morning   Finally   A week later

Revenge is sweet
a) *One day*
b) ____
c) ____
d) ____
e) ____

Dinner by post
1 *Last year*
2 ____
3 ____
4 ____
5 ____
6 ____

2 Work with a partner. Choose a story. Take it in turns and use the time adverbials in 1 to retell the story *without* looking at the text on page 74.

Lexis: adverbs of manner

1 Work with a partner. Complete the tables with an adverb or adjective from the stories on page 74.

Revenge is sweet

Adjective	Adverb
a) unhappy	*unhappily*
b) ____	badly
c) ____	angrily
d) quick	____
e) ____	beautifully
f) careful	____
g) quiet	____

Dinner by post

Adjective	Adverb
1 *different*	differently
2 early	____
3 late	____
4 ____	tidily
5 ____	attractively
6 ____	well
7 loud	____

2 Work with a partner. Use the information in the tables in 1 to answer the questions on adverb formation.

a) How do you make adverbs from most adjectives?
b) How do you make adverbs from adjectives ending in *y*?
c) What are the adverbs for the adjectives *good, early, late*?

3 Re-write these sentences in the usual order.

subject + verb + object + adverb

a) I slowly eat very food my   *I   eat   my food   very slowly.*
b) I very drive car quickly my
c) I days plan my carefully very
d) I play badly guitar the very
e) I my money spend very intelligently
f) I for arrive very appointments early
g) I phone talk the on very quietly
h) I speak very well English

4 How many sentences in 3 are true for you? Re-write the sentences so that they are all true for you. Compare your sentences with a partner.

Punctuation

1 Work with a partner. Re-write the story with the correct punctuation and capital letters.

> a shoplifter was trying to steal a watch from an exclusive jewellery shop when the manager caught him
>
> please dont call the police Ill buy the watch said the shoplifter
>
> the manager thought about it for a moment and then said well okay thats 500 dollars
>
> oh dear said the shoplifter thats more than I planned to spend can you show me something less expensive

2 Work with a partner. You are going to read another story called *Usher's revenge*. Look at the pictures and follow the instructions.

- Find out the meaning of the expressions in the box. Use a dictionary.
- Discuss what you think happens in the story.
- Student A turn to page 93. Student B turn to page 105.

> mystery play   stage   usher   tip   front row   whisper

Close up

Past continuous

Language reference p77

Verb structures p114

1 Work with a partner. Look at this sentence from the story *Revenge is sweet* on page 74. Discuss the questions.

One day <u>she was driving</u> home when <u>she saw</u> his car parked outside his lover's house.

a) Which <u>underlined</u> verb is in the past simple tense? Which <u>underlined</u> verb is in the past continuous tense?

b) Which tense do you use to describe something that was in progress when another event happened?

c) Which tense do you use to describe an event that happened at a particular moment?

2 Work with a partner. Complete the questions and write two possible answers.

a) *Were* you living in the same house this time last year?   *Yes, I was.*   *No, I wasn't.*

b) *Were* your parents watching TV at 11.30 last night?   *Yes, they* ____   *No, they* ____

c) ____ you having an English lesson this time yesterday?   ____   ____

d) ____ it raining when you woke up this morning?   ____   ____

e) ____ you wearing a hat when you went out this morning?   ____   ____

f) ____ you speaking English when the lesson started?   ____   ____

3 🔘 **91** Listen, check and repeat. Work with a partner. Ask and answer the questions in 2. Discuss your answers.

Once upon a time

Writing a story

1 Work with a partner. The pictures illustrate a modern fairy tale. Match the words in the box to the appropriate pictures and discuss what the story is about.

a frog   a castle   children   a beautiful princess   an evil witch
a handsome prince   a kiss   a pond   clothes

2 Work in groups of three to five. You are going to write the story. Discuss answers to the questions in column A, and discuss ways of completing the sentence beginnings in column B. Give your story a title.

Have you ever heard the story of the princess and the frog?
Well, once upon a time, there was a princess. ...

A	B
a) What kind of person was the princess?	She was ...
b) Where did she live?	She lived in ...
c) Where was she sitting?	One day, she was sitting ...
d) What was she thinking about?	She was thinking about ...
e) Who did she meet?	There she met ...
f) What did he say to her?	He said to her, ...
g) What happened later?	Later, ...

3 [cassette] **92** Listen to the original story and compare it with your own. What are the differences?

4 Listen again to the original story and answer the questions in column A in 2.

5 Work with the class. Compare stories and decide which ending is the best one.

Extreme

Reading

1 You are going to read and listen to a poem. Before you read the poem, match each of the word lists *A–D* to the photographs *1–4*. Find the meaning of each word. Use your dictionary if necessary. For example: *A–3*.

A	B	C	D
fields a <u>ri</u>ver clouds a <u>rain</u>bow	a <u>de</u>sert stars <u>pla</u>nets space	snow ice a <u>gla</u>cier	a vol<u>ca</u>no sea cliffs

2 📼 **93** Read and listen to the poem. What do you think the correct title is?

a) *I hate Geography*
b) *I love Geography*
c) *I don't mind Geography*

3 Work with a partner. Which geographical features in the pictures in 1 can you see in your country? Where?

Word & sentence stress

1 The poem above has a very regular stress pattern. <u>Underline</u> the stressed syllables on each line.

2 📼 **94** Listen and repeat the poem at the same time as the recording. Keep in time with the beat.

3 📼 **95** Listen and say the poem in time with the beat.

I ____ Geography

Other <u>peo</u>ple, <u>oth</u>er <u>pla</u>ces,
<u>Dif</u>ferent <u>cus</u>toms, <u>dif</u>ferent <u>fac</u>es,
Drought and desert, field and plain,
Snow and ice and monsoon rain,
5 Volcanoes, glaciers,
Bubbling springs,
Clouds and rainbows,
Countless things.
Stars and planets, distant space,
10 Whatever's ugly, full of grace.
Seas and rivers,
Cliffs and caves,
The wondrous ways this world behaves.
So much to learn; so much to know;
15 And so much farther still to go.

by John Kitching

Extreme hotels

1 Work with a partner. You are going to read an article about a hotel in Sweden. Match the figures in column A with the probable meanings in column B. Then read the article and check your answers.

A	B
40,000	= Year the first hotel was constructed.
1990	= Temperature in Celsius inside the hotel.
64	= Tons of ice and snow used to build the hotel.
14,000	= Temperature in Celsius outside the hotel.
-30	= Number of rooms in the hotel.
-5	= Number of hotel guests last year.

THE COOLEST
HOTEL IN THE WORLD

Can you imagine a hotel that is entirely made of ice? Well, it exists in Sweden, but only in winter. In spring, the hotel melts away and disappears into the river.

5 The Ice Hotel is situated on the shores of the Torne River in the old village of Jukkasjarvi, Sweden.

Every winter, work starts on building a new Ice Hotel, involving 40,000 tons of ice and snow. 10,000 tons of ice is taken from the Torne River, 10 and 30,000 tons of snow is provided by Mother Nature.

The first Ice Hotel was constructed in 1990. It started as a single room – now it has 64 rooms, as well as an Ice Chapel, an art gallery, a cinema, a 15 theatre and an Absolut Ice Bar. Last winter, more than 14,000 guests spent the night at the Ice Hotel.

Outside, the temperature is -30°C, but inside the hotel, the temperature is always around -5°C. All the furniture is made of ice, including the beds, 20 but nobody gets cold. The beds are covered with reindeer skins and guests are given warm clothes and special arctic sleeping bags.

In the Absolut Ice Bar, the drinks are served in glasses made of ice, so there is no need for ice 25 cubes!

Every year the interior of the hotel is designed by different artists from all over the world. It is described by visitors as 'absolutely stunning', 'one of the most beautiful places I've ever seen' 30 and 'unique'.

2 Work with a partner. Answer the questions about the Ice Hotel.

a) Where is it situated?
b) What is it built of?
c) What is the furniture made of?
d) What are the beds covered with?
e) Who is the interior designed by?
f) How is it described by visitors?

3 Answer the questions in 2 for a building you know well. Tell your partner about the building.

For example: *The Guggenheim Museum is situated near the river Nervion in Bilbao. It's built of metal and …*

Close up

Passives   **1**   Work with a partner. Look at the active and passive sentences below and answer the questions.

Active				**Passive**		
subject	verb	object		subject	verb	
Somebody	constructed	the first Ice Hotel	in 1990.	The first Ice Hotel	was constructed	in 1990.
subject	verb	object		subject	verb	
Somebody	takes	ice	from the Torne River.	Ice	is taken	from the Torne River.

a) Find the objects of the active sentences. Are they: (1) before the verb; (2) after the verb?

b) Find the same words in the passive sentences? Are they: (1) before the verb; (2) after the verb?

c) True or false? The object of an active sentence becomes the subject of a passive sentence.

d) Look at the first word of the verb in the passive sentences. Is it a form of: (1) *be*; (2) *do*; (3) *have*?

e) Look at the second word. Is it in: (1) the infinitive; (2) the past simple; (3) the past participle?

f) True or false? Passive verbs consist of a form of *be* plus a past participle.

g) Read all the sentences. Does *somebody* appear in the active or the passive sentences?

h) Do we know who *somebody* is?

i) True or false? We can use the passive to talk about actions when we don't know who performed them.

2   Work with a partner. Complete the questions and write two possible answers.

a)	*Was* your house built before 1980?	Yes, it *was*.	No, it *wasn't*.
b)	*Were* your shoes designed in Italy?	Yes, they ___	No, they ___
c)	*Is* your salary paid by cheque?	Yes, ___	No, ___
d)	___ you invited to any parties last week?	___	___
e)	___ your name spelt the same way in English?	___	___
f)	___ your mobile phone made in Japan?	___	___

3   ▭ 96 Listen, check and repeat. Work with a partner. Ask and answer the questions in 2. Discuss your answers.

Language reference: passives

In passive sentences, the object of the active verb becomes the subject of the passive verb.

Active				**Passive**		
subject	verb	object		subject	verb	
Somebody	constructed	the first Ice Hotel	in 1990.	The first Ice Hotel	was constructed	in 1990.

The passive is formed with *be* (*am, is, are, was, were*) + past participle (*constructed, taken*, etc. – see *Irregular verbs* on page 117). We can use the passive to talk about actions when we don't know who performed them.

*My shoes **were designed** in Italy.   All the furniture **is made** of ice.*

What's the weather like?

Lexis: the weather   **1**   Complete the chart with appropriate words.

	☀	☁☁☁	☁☁	〰〰	🌬	❄❄❄	⛈
Noun	(1) *sun*	cloud	(3) ____	fog	(5) ____	snow	(7) ____
Adjective/ Phrase	It's sunny. It's fine/dry. It's warm/ hot.	It's (2) ____ . It's dull.	It's rainy/wet. It's raining.	It's (4) ____ .	It's windy.	It's (6) ____ . It's snowing. It's cold/ freezing.	It's stormy.

2   Read the winter weather forecast for the North Pole. Would you like to go there? Tell your partner.

> ## THE NORTH POLE IN WINTER
>
> Today will start off <u>extremely cold</u> with temperatures of <u>minus 30</u> degrees Celsius. It will be <u>very windy</u> in the afternoon, and there will probably be <u>a snow storm</u> later on. It will be <u>dark</u> all day. Tomorrow will be the same, and the next day, and the day after. Summer might be a bit <u>warmer</u>, but not much.

3   📼 97 Work with a partner. Invent a winter weather forecast for London by replacing the <u>underlined</u> words and phrases in 2. Listen and compare your ideas.

Lexis: *will & might*   **1**   Complete these predictions about the weather.

> Verb structures p115

a)   The south have better weather than the north. (will)
   The south will have better weather than the north.
b)   Tomorrow probably be warmer than today. (will)
c)   I think we have a lot of snow next winter. (will)
d)   It rain later today. (might)
e)   There be a storm before the weekend. (might)
f)   It be sunny tomorrow. (won't)

will happen

↓

won't happen

2   Re-write the sentences so that they are true for where you live. Compare with a partner.

Anecdote   **1**   📼 98 You are going to listen to a woman talking about her favourite time of year. Listen and <u>underline</u> the answers she gives.

☐ Which months of the year do you like best?   a)   I like … (August, December, October, etc.)
☐ What season is that in your country?   b)   It's … (spring, summer, autumn, winter)
☐ What is the weather like at that time of year?   c)   It's … (warm but not hot, very sunny, cold, etc.)
☐ What's the countryside like at that time of year?   d)   The countryside is … (green, colourful, snowy, etc.)
☐ What do you usually wear at that time of year?   e)   I usually wear … (light clothes, smart clothes, etc.)
☐ What do you usually do at that time of the year?   f)   I go … (skiing, to the beach, for walks in the hills, etc.)
☐ What do you particularly like about that time of year?   g)   I like it because … (I'm on holiday / it's beautiful, etc.)

2   Think about your favourite time of the year. You are going to tell your partner about it. Read the questions and sentence beginnings in 1 again and think about what to say and how to say it.

3   Tell your partner about your favourite time of year.

Experiences

> **Language reviewed:** present perfect (Unit 16); computers (Unit 16); driving (Unit 17); past participles (Unit 16); past continuous (Unit 18); question forms (Unit 17)

Present perfect

Work with a partner. You are going to find out about your partner's experience with computers and with driving.

- Complete each question with the past participle of the verb in brackets.
- Complete the *Me* column with *Yes* or *No* and guess the answers for you partner.
- Ask the questions and find out if you were right about your partner's experience.

Questions	Me	Partner
Computer experience		
a) Have you ever (buy) anything on the internet? *bought*		
b) Have you ever (download) music from the internet?		
c) Have you ever (go) to an online auction?		
d) Have you ever (delete) an important file by mistake?		
e) Have you ever (set up) a website?		
f) Have you ever (take part) in a chat-room discussion?		
Driving experience		
g) Have you ever (be) late because of a traffic jam?		
h) Have you ever (drive) in a foreign country?		
i) Have you ever (have) a parking ticket?		
j) Have you ever (drive) at over 200kph?		
k) Have you ever (lend) your car to a friend?		
l) Have you ever (lose) your car keys?		

Word stress

1 Work with a partner. Say these words from Units 16–19 and <u>underline</u> the stressed syllable. In each group (circle) the word with a different stress pattern or different number of syllables from the other two.

a) <u>sce</u>nery (vol<u>ca</u>no) <u>dan</u>gerous
b) pro<u>nounced</u> <u>sur</u>face <u>hap</u>pened
c) pol<u>lu</u>tion <u>eve</u>ning <u>bus</u>iness
d) <u>de</u>sert de<u>lete</u> <u>con</u>cert
e) <u>an</u>grily <u>ti</u>dily <u>reg</u>ularly
f) conver<u>sa</u>tion ex<u>pres</u>sion prepo<u>si</u>tion

2 🔊 99 Listen, check and repeat the answers to 1.

Past participles

🔊 100 You are going to play bingo. Follow the instructions.

- Copy the bingo card and complete it with the past participle forms of nine different verbs in the box.
- Listen to the recording and when you hear a verb on your card, ~~cross it out~~.
- When three verbs in a vertical (↓), horizontal (→) or diagonal (↘) line are crossed out, shout, 'Bingo!'.
- Check your answers with the tapescript on page 127.

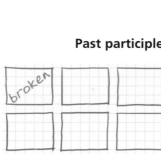

break	bring	build	catch	do	drive	eat	fall	feel	find	have	hear
keep	lend	make	mean	meet	pay	read	sell	shoot	sit	sleep	
speak	spend	teach	think	wake	wear	write					

Past simple & past continuous

1 Work with a partner. Complete the story with the verb forms in the box. Predict the ending of the story.

> didn't come   continued   ~~was filming~~   found   gave   was planning
> shook   was talking   went   went

A Hollywood director (1) *was filming* an important film in the desert when an old Native American man (2) ____ up to him and said, 'Tomorrow rain.'
The next day it rained.

A few days later, the director (3) ____ to the cameraman about the next day's filming. The Native American went up to him and said, 'Tomorrow storm.'

He was right again, and he saved the director thousands of dollars.

The director was very impressed and (4) ____ the old man a job.

The old man (5) ____ to predict the weather correctly, but then he (6) ____ for three weeks.

The director (7) ____ to film an important scene and he needed good weather. So he (8) ____ to look for the Native American.

When he (9) ____ the old man, he said, 'Listen, I have to film an important scene tomorrow. What will the weather be like?'

The old man (10) ____ his head and said, '.........'

2 🎞 **101** Listen and check your answers and ideas in 1.

Anecdote   **1** Complete the Anecdote questions with *How*, *What*, *When*, *Where* and *Who*.

☐ 1 ____ did your journey start and finish?   It was from my house to … (school, my grandparents', etc.)
☐ 2 ____ far was it?   It was … (3 kilometres, 85 kilometres, 370 kilometres, etc.)
☐ 3 ____ did you travel?   I went … (on foot, by bike, by car, by bus, by train, etc.)
☐ 4 ____ time did you usually set off?   I usually set off … (at eight o'clock, after school, very early, etc.)
☐ 5 ____ long did it take you?   It took me … (half an hour, six hours, all day, etc.)
☐ 6 ____ sort of countryside did you go through?   I went … (through woods, along the coast, down a hill, etc.)
☐ 7 ____ sort of buildings did you go past?   I went past … (a church, a supermarket, a monument, etc.)
☐ 8 ____ did you usually travel with?   I travelled … (with my family, with my friends, alone, etc.)
☐ 9 ____ did you usually do on your journey?   I … (looked out of the window, slept, listened to music, etc.)
☐ 10 ____ was the last time you did this journey?   It was … (in 1995, three months ago, etc.)

2 🎞 **102** Think about a journey that you did many times when you were younger. You are going to tell a partner about it. Read and listen to the questions and think about your answers.

3 Think about what to say and how to say it. Use the sentence beginnings to help you.

4 Tell your partner about your journey.

Language reviewed:
All the main structures in *Inside Out* Elementary.

The Revision Game

7
Talk about an old school friend.

8
I've got too much work.
(page 61)

9
I've been to Paris three years ago.
(page 69)

10
How long it does take you to get to work?
(page 71)

6
Had you a good day yesterday?
(page 40)

FINISH

5
How many rice is there?
(page 29)

4
He likes it.
(page 17)

3
Talk about your house.

2
Do you be retired?
(page 12)

1
Have you got a car?
(page 9)

Player 1
START

3
Talk about your last summer holiday.

2
I hardly get up ever after 11am.
(page 15)

1
Do you live in London?
(page 12)

Player 4
START

4
She hates do the housework.
(page 17)

5
Are there any banks in this street?
(page 20)

6
Where did you be born?
(page 40)

FINISH

7
Talk about your favourite time of year.

8
I'm going have a big party.
(page 53)

9
You shouldn't work so late.
(page 61)

10
What time you get up?
(page 71)

Review 4

10
My shoes were designed in Italy.
(page 80)

9
He's met the love of his life in 1996.
(page 69)

8
The birds are singing?
(page 49)

7
Talk about the last time you went shopping.

FINISH

6
What you watched on TV last night?
(page 40)

5
We don't have to do any homework.
(page 32)

4
There's a lot pasta.
(page 29)

Player 2 START

1
Are you married?
(page 9)

2
Does your sister have got a job?
(page 12)

3
Talk about one of your relatives.

Player 3 START

1
Does he work in an office?
(page 12)

2
She sometimes is late for the lesson.
(page 15)

3
Talk about someone you think has a good job.

4
You can to smoke.
(page 32)

5
Did the weather be good yesterday?
(page 40)

6
I'd like to climb Mount Fuji in Japan.
(page 53)

FINISH

10
How many people can you get in your car?
(page 71)

9
It's not enough big.
(page 61)

8
I'm not as tall my father.
(page 57)

7
Talk about the last time you had a delicious meal.

HOW TO PLAY

Play the game with three, four or five players. One person in each game is the *Checker*. They don't play the game. You will need a coin and counters and an extra copy of *Inside Out* Elementary Student's Book.

1   Each player places their counter on a different square marked START.

2   Decide who is going to start the game. The first player tosses the coin and moves the counter along their 'road' as follows: 'Heads' = two spaces. 'Tails' = one space.

3   Players then play in turns. If a player lands on a grammar square (darker colour) they must decide if they think the sentence on that square is grammatically correct or incorrect. If they think the sentence is incorrect, they must correct it.

4   The *Checker* then turns to the Language reference on the page given to see if the player is right. If the player is right, they can wait for their next run. If the player is wrong, they miss a turn.

5   If a player lands on a speaking square (lighter colour), they must talk about the topic for sixty seconds. The *Checker* times the player from the moment they start speaking.

6   The first player to reach their FINISH is the winner.

Review 4

Pairwork: Student A

1 You

Page 7. Alphabet, 3

You and your partner have different lines of the same optician's 'eye chart'. Take it in turns to dictate your lines to each other to complete the chart. Check your answers.

1	A
2	__ __ __
3	E I B V A
4	__ __ __ __ __
5	I A U V B J G H
6	__ __ __ __ __ __ __

2 People

Page 10. Lexis: family words, 4

You have some information about Charlie Tait's family. Your partner has some information about Willie Tait's family. Take it in turns to read out your information. What are the five differences between the two families?

Charlie Tait's family	Willie Tait's family: same (✓) or different (✗)?
a) They live at number 24 Dover Street.	✗ 23 Dover Street
b) They've got three bedrooms.	✓
c) They've got a blue Renault Clio.	____
d) The registration number is W302 XBL.	____
e) Their phone number is 01792 880 761.	____
f) They go on holiday every year to Benidorm in Spain.	____
g) Their favourite meal is burger and chips.	____
h) Charlie's favourite drink is beer.	____

3 Days

Page 15. Close up. Adverbs of frequency, 2

You are going to compare habits with your partner. You are going to ask questions about the nighttime. Your partner is going to ask questions about the daytime.

- Complete the *Me* column with an adverb to make the sentences true for you.
- Ask your partner questions beginning: *Do you ever …?* and complete the *My partner* column.
  For example: *A: Do you ever read in bed?   B: Yes, sometimes.*
- Discuss your answers. Are you the same (✓) or different (✗)?

Night (and day)

Me	My partner	✓ = We're the same. ✗ = We're different.
a) I *never* read in bed.	He/She *sometimes* reads in bed.	✗
b) I ____ sleep with the windows open.	____	____
c) I ____ remember my dreams.	____	____
d) I ____ sleep more than seven hours.	____	____
e) I ____ wear pyjamas in bed.	____	____
f) I ____ sleep with the light on.	____	____
g) I ____ ?	____	____

Adverbs: always   usually   often   sometimes   hardly ever   never

3 Days

Page 17. Likes & dislikes, 4

You are going to find out how well you know your partner's likes and dislikes.

- Write your partner's name.
- Complete the sentences about him or her with phrases from the box.
- Ask questions to check your answers. See if you are right or wrong.
  A: Do you like going to night clubs?
  B: No, I hate it.
  A: Oh, I was wrong.

Partner's name: _____		✓ = I'm right. ✗ = I'm wrong.
a) *She really likes*	going to night clubs.	✗
b) ____	watching football.	____
c) ____	listening to reggae.	____
d) ____	getting up late.	____
e) ____	eating vegetables.	____
f) ____	playing cards.	____
g) ____	doing the ironing.	____
h) ____	staying in.	____

He/She   loves   really likes   likes   doesn't mind   doesn't like   hates

---

4 Living

Page 18. Reading, 5

Beckingham Palace (continued)

In the entrance hall of Beckingham Palace, there are two thrones – one for Victoria and one for David. Victoria and David often invite guests to Beckingham Palace, so there are seven bedrooms. Victoria's a singer, and David's a football player, so there's a recording studio for her and a football pitch for him! There's a bathroom dedicated to Audrey Hepburn, because Victoria is a fan of the actress. There's a children's playroom for their two children – all their favourite Disney characters are on the wall. It's easy to keep fit at Beckingham Palace because there's a gym and an indoor swimming pool.

---

4 Living

Page 19. Close up. *there is / there are*, 3

You and your partner have pictures of different living rooms. Complete the following tasks.

- Do <u>not</u> look at Student B's picture. Sit facing your partner. Ask questions to find at least six similarities in your pictures.

  For example:
  A: Is there a sofa in your picture?
  B: Yes, there is. / No, there isn't.
  A: Are there any cushions on the sofa?
  B: Yes, there are. / No, there aren't.

- When you have found six similarities, look at Student B's picture. Can you find any more similarities?

- Discuss these questions.
  a) What kind of house do you think these rooms are in?
  b) What kind of people do you think live in these houses?
  c) Do you like these rooms? Why? / Why not?

4 Living

Page 21. Writing

1   Read this postcard from Helen to her mum. How does she feel about her holiday? Compare your answer with Student B, but don't look at their postcard yet.

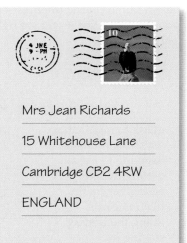

Dear Mum,

I'm having a <u>terrible</u> holiday. The hotel is <u>awful</u>, and my room is really <u>dirty</u>. There <u>aren't any</u> nice shops, and everything is really <u>expensive</u>. There are lots of restaurants, <u>but</u> the food is <u>horrible</u>.
   The people here are really <u>unfriendly</u>, and they <u>never</u> speak to you in the street.
   The weather is <u>cold</u> and <u>wet</u>. I feel really <u>miserable</u>, and I <u>want</u> to come home.

Love, Helen XXX

PS   Please can you put some money into my bank account?

Mrs Jean Richards

15 Whitehouse Lane

Cambridge CB2 4RW

ENGLAND

2   Re-write the postcard in 1. Replace the <u>underlined</u> words with words from the box to make the postcard sound positive.

| friendly ~~lovely~~ warm clean delicious and always dry |
| don't want wonderful cheap happy are some |

Dear Mum,

I'm having a lovely holiday. The hotel …

3   Compare your positive and negative postcards with Student B.

6 Food

Page 28. Close up. Quantity, 4

You are going to find out if your partner does similar things to you in a normal day.

*   Complete your questions with *much* or *many*.
*   Write your own answers to the questions in the column marked *Me*.
*   Ask Student B the questions. Write Student B's answers in the column marked *My partner*.
*   What are the similarities and differences between you and your partner?

Questions	Me	My partner
In a normal day …		
a) How ____ fruit do you eat?	____	____
b) How ____ coffee do you drink?	____	____
c) How ____ driving do you do?	____	____
d) How ____ sport do you watch on the TV?	____	____
e) How ____ money do you carry around?	____	____
f) How ____ time do you spend on the internet?	____	____

7 Work

Page 30. Lexis: describing character, 3

You are going to complete the table below with ten adjectives to describe character.

- Read out words *a–e* in the table. The stressed syllables are <u>underlined</u>.
- Student B will match a definition to each word and read it out.
- If you both agree, write the definition in your table. Use a dictionary if necessary.

Words	Definitions
a) shy	*I'm nervous about meeting people.*
b) <u>ho</u>nest	____
c) <u>friend</u>ly	____
d) <u>sen</u>sible	____
e) <u>con</u>fident	____
f) ____	____
g) ____	____
h) ____	____
i) ____	____
j) ____	____

- Change roles. Student B will read out words *f–j*. Match one of the definitions below to each word and read it out.
- The table is complete when you have all ten words with their ten definitions.

> **Definitions of Student B's words**
> I'm happy and I'm always smiling.   I like helping people.
> I understand things quickly and easily.   I understand other people's feelings.
> I'm relaxed. I never worry about anything.

7 Work

Page 31. Lexis: jobs, 2

Ask your partner questions to complete the questionnaire. Choose an appropriate job for them from the suggestions or your own ideas. Explain your choice to your partner. Give reasons.

Partner's name: ____

Are you ...	Yes	No	Sometimes	Possible jobs
practical?	____	____	____	a farmer
independent?	____	____	____	a computer programmer
creative?	____	____	____	a dancer
helpful?	____	____	____	a secondary school teacher
ambitious?	____	____	____	a politician
serious?	____	____	____	a lawyer
good at Maths?	____	____	____	
sporty?	____	____	____	____

Do you like ...	Yes	No	I don't mind	
working outside?	____	____	____	
solving problems?	____	____	____	
music and art?	____	____	____	*I think the best job for ____ is*
talking to people?	____	____	____	*____ because he/she is ____*
selling products?	____	____	____	*and he/she likes ____ .*
organising things?	____	____	____	
travelling?	____	____	____	
working in an office?	____	____	____	

8 Sea

Page 36. Close up. Past simple, 5

You are going to compare the first time you did something with the first time your partner did the same thing.

- Complete your questions with the past forms of the verbs in brackets.
- Write your own answers to the questions in the column marked *Me*.
- Ask Student B the questions. Write Student B's answers in the column marked *My partner*.
- What are the similarities and differences between you and your partner?

Questions	Me	My partner
a) When was the first time you (go) to a wedding?	____	____
b) When was the first time you (travel) alone?	____	____
c) When was the first time you (use) a credit card?	____	____
d) When was the first time you (speak) to a foreigner?	____	____
e) When was the first time you (drive) a car?	____	____
f) When was the first time you (earn) some money?	____	____

9 Solo

Page 40. Close up. Past simple, 4

You are going to ask and answer questions about pop singers.

- Write questions for the pop facts below.
- Ask Student B your questions.
- Answer Student B's questions using information in the box.

a) Bob Marley was from Jamaica. Where …? *Where was Bob Marley from?*
b) Robbie Williams left *Take That* to go solo in 1996. When …?
c) Björk was born in Iceland. Where …?
d) George Michael's original name was Giorgios Kyriacou Panayiotou. What …?
e) Kurt Cobain died in 1994. When …?
f) Madonna married Guy Ritchie in 2000. Who …?

1985   Anna Mae Bullock   The USA   1980   Canada   Priscilla Ann Beaulieu

11 Looks

Page 46. Lexis: description, 4

You are going to label the people in picture B. Their names are *Jason, Jane, Emma, Max* and *Mickey*. Your partner is going to label the people in picture A. Take it in turns to ask questions.

For example:
A: *Which one is Jason?*
B: *He's black. He's got short dark hair with blond highlights.*

Marco   Karen   Lily   Paul   Susanna

1 ____   2 ____   3 ____   4 ____   5 ____

11 Looks

Page 49. Close up. Present continuous, 3

You are going to mime three of the following activities. Your partner is going to mime different activities. Take it in turns to guess what your partner is miming.

a) You are eating an ice-cream.
b) You are watching a horror film.
c) You are doing the ironing.
d) You are putting on ski boots.
e) You are waiting to see the dentist.
f) You are having a cold shower.

12 Reality

Page 52. Close up. *(be) going to*, 5

You and your partner are going to compare your plans for the immediate future.

• Answer the questions and complete the *Me* column with a ✓, ✗, or ? according to the key.
• Ask your partner the same questions and complete the *My partner* column.
• Discuss your answers. Are you more sure or less sure about your plans than your partner?

Questions	Me	My partner	Key
a) Are you going to walk home after class?	____	____	✓ = Yes, I am.
b) Are you going to send any emails this evening?	____	____	✗ = No, I'm not.
c) Are you going to have lunch at home tomorrow?	____	____	? = I'm not sure.
d) Are you going to go out on Saturday night?	____	____	
e) Are you going to do any studying in the next few days?	____	____	
f) Are you going to go anywhere interesting next week?	____	____	

13 Things

Page 56. Close up. Superlatives, 2

You are going to do a quiz about your town/city.

• Complete the questions with the correct superlative form and add a question of your own.
• Answer the questions with your own ideas in the *Me* column.
• Ask your partner the questions and write your partner's answers in the *My partner* column.
• Discuss your ideas.

Town/City quiz

Questions	Me	My partner
a) Which is the (ugly) *ugliest* building?	____	____
b) Which is the (famous) park?	____	____
c) Which is the (old) monument?	____	____
d) Which is the (expensive) street?	____	____
e) Which is the (big) supermarket?	____	____
f) Which is the (popular) pub or bar?	____	____
g) Which is the ____?	____	____

14 Energy

Page 59. Lexis: frequency expressions, 3

You are going to compare good and bad habits with your partner. You are going to ask your partner about good habits. Your partner is going to ask you about bad habits.

- Complete the *Me* column with frequency expressions to make the sentences true for you.
- Ask your partner questions beginning: *How often …?* and complete the *My partner* column.
  For example: *A: How often do you do some exercise?   B: Twice a week.*
- Discuss your answers. Are you and your partner the same (✓) or different (✗)?

Good habits

Me	My partner	✓ = We're the same. ✗ = We're different.
a) I do some exercise ____ .	____	____
b) I eat fruit ____ .	____	____
c) I drink water ____ .	____	____
d) I have a holiday ____ .	____	____
e) I go to the dentist ____ .	____	____
f) I listen to relaxing music ____ .	____	____

16 dotcom

Page 67. Reading

You are going to find out about how two old school friends got back in touch with each other.

- Read the two emails and fill in the gaps using the words in the box. Check your answers with Student B.

band	cassette	Darren	garage	Pamela	party	phone	Purple

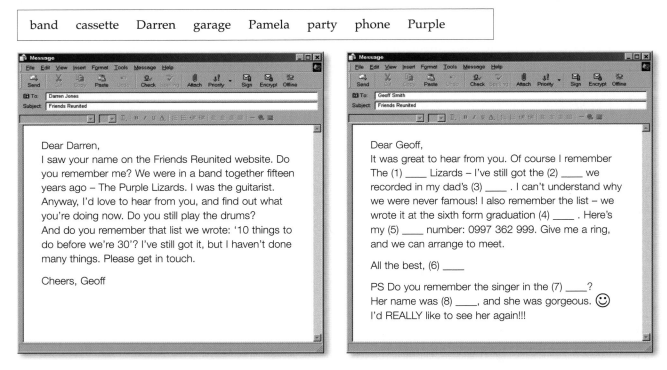

Dear Darren,
I saw your name on the Friends Reunited website. Do you remember me? We were in a band together fifteen years ago – The Purple Lizards. I was the guitarist. Anyway, I'd love to hear from you, and find out what you're doing now. Do you still play the drums?
And do you remember that list we wrote: '10 things to do before we're 30'? I've still got it, but I haven't done many things. Please get in touch.

Cheers, Geoff

Dear Geoff,
It was great to hear from you. Of course I remember The (1) ____ Lizards – I've still got the (2) ____ we recorded in my dad's (3) ____ . I can't understand why we were never famous! I also remember the list – we wrote it at the sixth form graduation (4) ____ . Here's my (5) ____ number: 0997 362 999. Give me a ring, and we can arrange to meet.

All the best, (6) ____

PS Do you remember the singer in the (7) ____?
Her name was (8) ____, and she was gorgeous. ☺
I'd REALLY like to see her again!!!

- You and your partner have alternate lines of a summary of the email exchange. Complete the summary with your own ideas first and then check with your partner.

a) Geoff saw Darren's
b) *name on the Friends Reunited*
c) website. They played in a
d) ____
e) guitarist and Darren played
f) ____
g) list: '10 things to
h) ____
i) Geoff to give him a
j) ____ .

- When was the last time you got in touch with an old friend? Tell your partner.

16 dotcom

Page 69. Close up. Present perfect, 4

You are going to talk to your partner about things you've both done.

- Complete the *Me* column to make the sentences true for you. Add one sentence of your own.
- Ask your partner questions beginning: *What's the ...?* and complete the *My partner* column.
  For example: *A: What's the best website you've ever visited? B: Er, probably the BBC one. It's amazing.*
- Discuss your answers.

Me	My partner
a) The best website I've ever visited is ____ . b) The best book I've ever read is ____ . c) The best party I've ever been to is ____ . d) The best-looking woman I've ever seen is ____ . e) The best meal I've ever had is ____ . f) The most dangerous sport I've ever tried is ____ . g) ____ .	The best website he/she's visited is ____ . ____ ____ ____ ____ ____ ____

17 Drive

Page 71. Close up. Questions with *How* + adverb/adjective & *What* + noun, 3

You are going to ask questions and compare information about you and your partner.

- Read the *Who* questions in column A, and complete the *How* and *What* questions in column B which will give you the information you want about you and your partner.
- Ask your partner the questions in column B and (circle) the appropriate answer (*Me* or *My partner*) in column A.
- Compare your answers with other students. Find out the answer to each question in column A for the class.

A: Who ...? – Me or my partner?	B
a) Who travels by train the most? (*Me / My partner*) b) Who gets up earliest in the morning? (*Me / My partner*) c) Who has the fastest car? (*Me / My partner*) d) Who spends the most money on travelling every week? (*Me / My partner*) e) Who lives the furthest from the school? (*Me / My partner*) f) Who takes the longest to get to work/school? (*Me / My partner*)	How often *do you travel by train?* What time ___? How fast ___? How much ___? How far ___? How long ___?

18 Justice

Page 76. Punctuation, 2

You have some lines of the story, *Usher's revenge*, and Student B has the other lines.

- Take it in turns to dictate your lines to each other including punctuation and capital letters.
- Complete and then compare your stories. They should be identical.
- What was the usher's revenge?

Usher's revenge
A: A man arrived at the theatre
B: ____
A: but his seat was too far
B: ____
A: So he said to the usher,
B: ____
A: and I'll give you a generous tip."
B: ____
A: and the man gave him 25 cents.
B: ____
A: and then he bent down and whispered to the man,
B: ____

Additional material

6 Food

Page 27. Reading & listening, 4

1   Write the following information in the shapes below and opposite.

- Food you love.
- Food you hate.
- Something you are really good at cooking.
- The name of your favourite restaurant.
- A hot drink you like.
- A cold drink you like.
- A drink you don't like.
- The name of somebody you know who cooks really well.
- Your favourite ice-cream flavour: vanilla, chocolate, banana, strawberry …
- The name of somebody you'd like to have a meal with.

2   Compare with a partner. Explain and talk about the information in your shapes.

7 Work

Page 30. Lexis: describing character, 4

a   *Qualities*: sensitive, clever, honest.
You can be alone for a long time without being bored.

b   *Qualities*: independent, creative, confident.
You're different – you're not one of the crowd.

c   *Qualities*: energetic, sociable, adventurous.
You don't like routine. You like to do something different every day.

d   *Qualities*: sensible, kind, helpful.
You love animals and nature.

e   *Qualities*: confident, hard-working, ambitious.
You're successful at work. You want to get to the top of your profession.

f   *Qualities*: practical, friendly, independent.
You like travelling to beautiful places.

g   *Qualities*: cheerful, easy-going, sociable.
You enjoy going out and meeting new people.

h   *Qualities*: romantic, sensitive, shy.
Your listen to your heart, not your head. You think it is important to have dreams.

i   *Qualities*: serious, honest, confident.
You love art, literature and theatre. You do not follow fashion.

8 Sea

Page 37. Reading & writing, 3

Work with a partner. You are going to write the story of a disastrous trip to see a football match.

- Look at the pictures and discuss what you think happened in the story.
- Complete the sentences (*a–i*) by putting the verbs in the past simple form.
- Match each sentence with a picture and write the completed story.

1 Harry and Joss were Manchester United fans. One day, …

2 The next day, …

3 Then, …

4 Two weeks later, …

5 At first, …

6 But after a few hours …

7 Suddenly, …

8 Eventually, …

9 Two days later, …

a)   … they (enjoy) the flight. They (have) lunch, (read) the newspapers and (sleep) for a short time.

b)   … they (go) to the travel agents and booked flights to Santiago.

c)   … they (watch) the match in a hotel bar.

d)   *Harry and Joss were Manchester United fans. One day,* they (decide) *decided* to travel to Spain to watch Manchester United play against the Spanish team, Deportivo La Coruña.   *1*

e)   … they (realise) their mistake.

f)   … Joss (ask) how long the flight to Santiago was. The flight attendant (say) 'Eleven hours, sir. South America's a long way from Manchester.'

g)   … they (look) at a map of Spain and (find) the nearest airport – Santiago.

h)   … they (travel) to Manchester airport. Their flight (be) on time.

i)   … they (arrive) in Santiago – but it wasn't Santiago in Spain. It (be) Santiago in Chile!

9 Solo

Page 39. Reading, 2

After two weeks, Andrew left the race because he was frightened of the ocean. Debra didn't want to stop the race and she decided to continue. She rowed the remaining 2,290 miles alone. The journey took 113 days. Debra arrived in Barbados seventy days after the winning team, but for most people she was the hero of the race. The Editor of *The Times* wrote on 28th January, 'The winner of the race is the girl that came last'.

11 Looks

Page 48. Reading 3

1 b 2 a 3 c 4 a 5 c 6 b 7 b 8 b 9 c 10 b 11 a 12 c

12 Reality

Page 52. Close up. *want to, 'd (would) like to, hope to*, 3

Work in groups of three. Choose five pictures (or draw your own in box *l*) and tell your partners how they represent your dreams.

13 Things

Page 54. Reading, 2

The top ten things (in order)

1 Money	3 TV Remote	5 Wedding ring	7 Reading glasses	9 Mobile phone
2 Keys	4 Gloves	6 Bag	8 Address book	10 Pet

13 Things

Page 54. Listening, 3

Work with a partner and follow the instructions.

- Match the descriptions (*a–l*) to the bags (*1–9*). Each description may refer to more than one bag.
- Take it in turns to choose a bag.
- Ask questions like the questions in Listening 2 on page 54 to find out which bag your partner chose.

a) It's brown and white check.   *4*
b) It's a shopping bag.
c) It's got a long strap.
d) It's huge.
e) It's a laptop bag.
f) It's made of plastic.
g) It's got some clothes in it.
h) It's got the letters CD on the handle.
i) It's made of leather.
j) It's not very big.
k) It's black with a white stripe.
l) It's got two pockets on the front.

Pairwork: Student B

1 You

Page 7. Alphabet, 3

You and your partner have different lines of the same optician's 'eye chart'. Take it in turns to dictate your lines to each other to complete the chart. Check your answers.

1	‾
2	C I H
3	_ _ _ _ _
4	G O J A Y E
5	_ _ _ _ _ _ _
6	W X A E Y O Q J Z

2 People

Page 10. Lexis: family words, 4

You have some information about Willie Tait's family. Your partner has some information about Charlie Tait's family. Take it in turns to read out your information. What are the five differences between the two families?

Willie Tait's family	Charlie Tait's family: same (✓) or different (✗)?
a) They live at number 23 Dover Street.	✗ 24 Dover Street
b) They've got three bedrooms.	✓
c) They've got a green Renault Clio.	____
d) The registration number is W303 XBL.	____
e) Their phone number is 01792 800 761.	____
f) They go on holiday every year to Benidorm in Spain.	____
g) Their favourite meal is burger and chips.	____
h) Willie's favourite drink is cider.	____

3 Days

Page 15. Close up. Adverbs of frequency, 2

You are going to compare habits with your partner. You are going to ask questions about the daytime. Your partner is going to ask questions about the nighttime.

- Complete the *Me* column with an adverb to make the sentences true for you.
- Ask your partner questions beginning: *Do you ever …?* and complete the *My partner* column.
  For example: *A: Do you ever get up before 7am?   B: Yes, sometimes.*
- Discuss your answers. Are you the same (✓) or different (✗)?

Day (and night) Me	My partner	✓ = We're the same. ✗ = We're different.
a) I *never* get up before 7am.	He/She *sometimes* gets up before 7am.	✗
b) I ____ have black coffee for breakfast.	____	____
c) I ____ walk to work/school.	____	____
d) I ____ meet friends for lunch.	____	____
e) I ____ make dinner for the family.	____	____
f) I ____ go to bed before midnight.	____	____
g) I ____ ?	____	____

Adverbs: always   usually   often   sometimes   hardly ever   never

3 Days
Page 17. Likes & dislikes, 4

You are going to find out how well you know your partner's likes and dislikes.

* Write your partner's name.
* Complete the sentences about him or her with phrases from the box.
* Ask questions to check your answers. See if you are right or wrong.
  A: Do you like going to parties?
  B: Yes, I love it.
  A: Yes, I'm right.

Partner's name: ____		✓ = I'm right. ✗ = I'm wrong.
a) *He really likes*	going to parties.	✓
b) ____	watching tennis.	____
c) ____	listening to jazz.	____
d) ____	getting up early.	____
e) ____	eating fish.	____
f) ____	playing computer or video games.	____
g) ____	doing the washing up.	____
h) ____	going out.	____

He/She   loves   really likes   likes   doesn't mind   doesn't like   hates

4 Living
Page 18. Reading, 5

Buckingham Palace (continued)
Buckingham Palace is the Queen's official residence. There are 609 rooms, and 700 staff work at the Palace. Tourists can visit the Palace in August and September and see paintings by Rembrandt, Rubens and Vermeer. Visitors can also enjoy a walk in the garden with its beautiful 19th century lake. The largest room in Buckingham Palace is the ballroom. It's 37 metres long, 18 metres wide and over 13 metres high. The Queen uses the throne room for special occasions and royal ceremonies.

4 Living
Page 19. Close up. *there is / there are*, 3

You and your partner have pictures of different living rooms. Complete the following tasks.

* Do <u>not</u> look at Student A's picture. Sit facing your partner. Ask questions to find at least six similarities in your pictures.

  For example:
  A: Is there a sofa in your picture?
  B: Yes, there is. / No, there isn't.
  A: Are there any cushions on the sofa?
  B: Yes, there are. / No, there aren't.

* When you have found six similarities, look at Student A's picture. Can you find any more similarities?

* Discuss these questions.

  a) What kind of house do you think these rooms are in?
  b) What kind of people do you think live in these houses?
  c) Do you like these rooms? Why? / Why not?

4 Living

Page 21. Writing

1   Read this postcard from Helen to her mum. How does she feel about her holiday? Compare your answer with Student A, but don't look at their postcard yet.

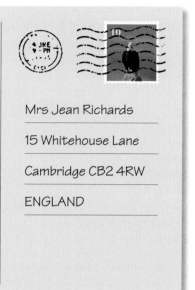

Dear Mum,

I'm having a <u>lovely</u> holiday. The hotel is <u>wonderful</u>, and my room is really <u>clean</u>. There <u>are some</u> nice shops, and everything is really <u>cheap</u>. There are lots of restaurants, <u>and</u> the food is <u>delicious</u>.

The people here are really <u>friendly</u>, and they <u>always</u> speak to you in the street.

The weather is <u>warm</u> and <u>dry</u>. I feel really <u>happy</u>, and I <u>don't want</u> to come home.

Love, Helen XXX

PS Please can you put some money into my bank account?

Mrs Jean Richards

15 Whitehouse Lane

Cambridge CB2 4RW

ENGLAND

2   Re-write the postcard in 1. Replace the <u>underlined</u> words with words from the box to make the postcard sound negative.

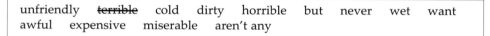

unfriendly   ~~terrible~~   cold   dirty   horrible   but   never   wet   want
awful   expensive   miserable   aren't any

Dear Mum,

I'm having a terrible holiday. The hotel ...

3   Compare your positive and negative postcards with Student A.

6 Food

Page 28. Close up. Quantity, 4

You are going to find out if your partner does similar things to you in a normal day.

* Complete your questions with *much* or *many*.
* Write your own answers to the questions in the column marked *Me*.
* Ask Student A the questions. Write Student A's answers in the column marked *My partner*.
* What are the similarities and differences between you and your partner?

Questions	Me	My partner
In a normal day ...		
a) How ____ phone calls do you make?	____	____
b) How ____ different people do you see or meet?	____	____
c) How ____ times do you use English?	____	____
d) How ____ shops do you go into?	____	____
e) How ____ CDs do you listen to?	____	____
f) How ____ keys do you carry around?	____	____

7 Work

Page 30. Lexis: describing character, 3

You are going to complete the table below with ten adjectives to describe character.

- Student A will read out words *a–e* in the table. Match one of the definitions below to each word and read it out.
- If you both agree, write the word and definition in your table. Use a dictionary if necessary.

> **Definitions of Student A's words**
> I always tell the truth. I never lie.   I'm never silly. I never do stupid things.
> I'm nervous about meeting people.   I'm sure about my own ideas and qualities.
> I'm kind and pleasant to other people.

- Change roles. Read out words *f–j*. The stressed syllables are <u>underlined</u>.
- Student A will match a definition to each word and read it out.
- The table is complete when you have all ten words with their ten definitions.

Words	Definitions
a) ____	____
b) ____	____
c) ____	____
d) ____	____
e) ____	____
f) easy-<u>go</u>ing	*I'm relaxed. I never worry about anything.*
g) <u>sen</u>sitive	____
h) <u>cheer</u>ful	____
i) <u>clev</u>er	____
j) <u>help</u>ful	____

7 Work

Page 31. Lexis: jobs, 2

Ask your partner questions to complete the questionnaire. Choose an appropriate job for them from the suggestions or your own ideas. Explain your choice to your partner. Give reasons.

Partner's name: ____

Are you ...	Yes	No	Sometimes	Possible jobs
practical?	____	____	____	a nurse
independent?	____	____	____	a scientist
creative?	____	____	____	a musician
helpful?	____	____	____	a sports instructor
ambitious?	____	____	____	a sales manager
serious?	____	____	____	a shop assistant
good at Maths?	____	____	____	____
sporty?	____	____	____	

Do you like ...	Yes	No	I don't mind	
working outside?	____	____	____	
solving problems?	____	____	____	
music and art?	____	____	____	*I think the best job for ____ is*
talking to people?	____	____	____	*____ because he/she is ____*
selling products?	____	____	____	*and he/she likes ____ .*
organising things?	____	____	____	
travelling?	____	____	____	
working in an office?	____	____	____	

8 Sea

Page 36. Close up. Past simple, 5

You are going to compare the last time you did something with the last time your partner did the same thing.

- Complete your questions with the past forms of the verbs in brackets.
- Write your own answers to the questions in the column marked *Me*.
- Ask Student A the questions. Write Student A's answers in the column marked *My partner*.
- What are the similarities and differences between you and your partner?

Questions	Me	My partner
a) When was the last time you (have) a haircut?	_____	_____
b) When was the last time you (telephone) your mother?	_____	_____
c) When was the last time you (make) dinner for someone?	_____	_____
d) When was the last time you (hold) a baby?	_____	_____
e) When was the last time you (give) a present to someone?	_____	_____
f) When was the last time you (take) a photograph?	_____	_____

9 Solo

Page 40. Close up. Past simple, 4

You are going to ask and answer questions about pop singers.

- Write questions for the pop facts below.
- Answer Student A's questions using information in the box.
- Ask Student A your questions.

a) Jimi Hendrix was from the USA. Where …? *Where was Jimi Hendrix from?*
b) Tina Turner's original name was Anna Mae Bullock. What …?
c) Celine Dion was born in Canada. Where …?
d) Sting left *The Police* to go solo in 1985. When …?
e) John Lennon died in 1980. When …?
f) Elvis Presley married Priscilla Ann Beaulieu in 1967. Who …?

1996 Iceland 1994 Giorgios Kyriacou Panayiotou Jamaica Guy Ritchie

11 Looks

Page 46. Lexis: description, 4

You are going to label the people in picture A. Their names are *Karen, Marco, Paul, Lily* and *Susanna*. Your partner is going to label the people in picture B. Take it in turns to ask questions.

For example:
A: *Which one is Karen?*
B: *She's got medium-length, straight hair. She's got big earrings.*

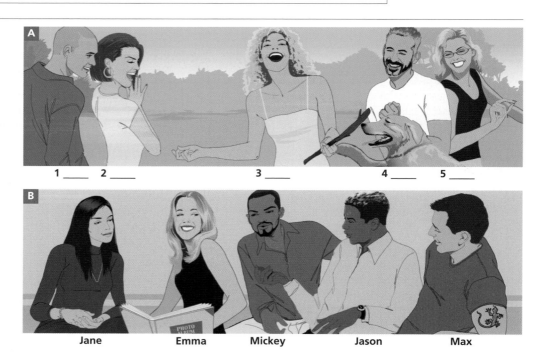

1 _____ 2 _____   3 _____   4 _____ 5 _____

Jane   Emma   Mickey   Jason   Max

11 Looks

Page 49. Close up. Present continuous, 3

You are going to mime three of the following activities. Your partner is going to mime different activities. Take it in turns to guess what your partner is miming.

a) You are eating spaghetti.
b) You are watching a funny film.
c) You are doing the washing up.
d) You are putting on lipstick.
e) You are waiting for a bus.
f) You are having a sauna.

12 Reality

Page 52. Close up. *(be) going to*, 5

You and your partner are going to compare your plans for the immediate future.

- Answer the questions and complete the *Me* column with a ✓, ✗, or ? according to the key.
- Ask your partner the same questions and complete the *My partner* column.
- Discuss your answers. Are you more sure or less sure about your plans than your partner?

Questions	Me	My partner	Key
a) Are you going to drive home after class?	____	____	✓ = Yes, I am.
b) Are you going to cook dinner this evening?	____	____	✗ = No, I'm not.
c) Are you going to have lunch in a restaurant tomorrow?	____	____	? = I'm not sure.
d) Are you going to go out on Friday night?	____	____	
e) Are you going to do any sport in the next few days?	____	____	
f) Are you going to do anything interesting next week?	____	____	

13 Things

Page 56. Close up. Superlatives, 2

You are going to do a quiz about your town/city.

- Complete the questions with the correct superlative form and add a question of your own.
- Answer the questions with your own ideas in the *Me* column.
- Ask your partner the questions and write your partner's answers in the *My partner* column.
- Discuss your ideas.

Town/City quiz

Questions	Me	My partner
a) Which is the (interesting) *most interesting* building?	____	____
b) Which is the (beautiful) park?	____	____
c) Which is the (modern) monument?	____	____
d) Which is the (busy) street?	____	____
e) Which is the (cheap) supermarket?	____	____
f) Which is the (quiet) pub or bar?	____	____
g) Which is the ____?	____	____

14 Energy

Page 59. Lexis: frequency expressions, 3

You are going to compare good and bad habits with your partner. You are going to ask your partner about bad habits. Your partner is going to ask you about good habits.

- Complete the *Me* column with frequency expressions to make the sentences true for you.
- Ask your partner questions beginning: *How often ...?* and complete the *My partner* column. For example: *A: How often do you arrive late for work/school?   B: Once a month.*
- Discuss your answers. Are you and your partner the same (✓) or different (✗)?

Bad habits

Me	My partner	✓ = We're the same. ✗ = We're different.
a) I arrive late for work/school ____ .	____	____
b) I eat fast food ____ .	____	____
c) I work late at night ____ .	____	____
d) I drink alcohol ____ .	____	____
e) I stay up all night ____ .	____	____
f) I get up late ____ .	____	____

16 dotcom

Page 67. Reading

You are going to find out about how two old school friends got back in touch with each other.

- Read the two emails and fill in the gaps using the words in the box. Check your answers with Student A.

30	drums	fifteen	Friends	Geoff	guitarist	list	Lizards

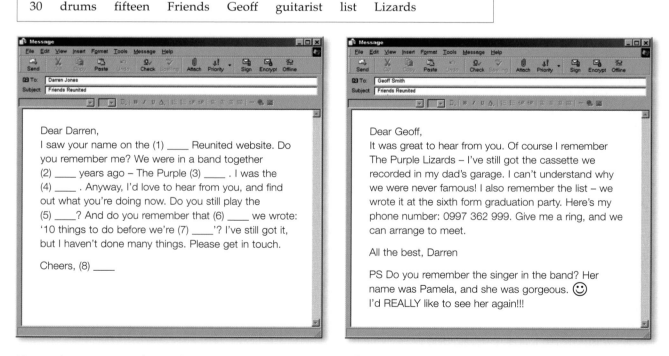

Dear Darren,
I saw your name on the (1) ____ Reunited website. Do you remember me? We were in a band together (2) ____ years ago – The Purple (3) ____ . I was the (4) ____ . Anyway, I'd love to hear from you, and find out what you're doing now. Do you still play the (5) ____? And do you remember that (6) ____ we wrote: '10 things to do before we're (7) ____'? I've still got it, but I haven't done many things. Please get in touch.

Cheers, (8) ____

Dear Geoff,
It was great to hear from you. Of course I remember The Purple Lizards – I've still got the cassette we recorded in my dad's garage. I can't understand why we were never famous! I also remember the list – we wrote it at the sixth form graduation party. Here's my phone number: 0997 362 999. Give me a ring, and we can arrange to meet.

All the best, Darren

PS Do you remember the singer in the band? Her name was Pamela, and she was gorgeous. ☺ I'd REALLY like to see her again!!!

- You and your partner have alternate lines of a summary of the email exchange. Complete the summary with your own ideas first and then check with your partner.

a) *Geoff saw Darren's*
b) name on the Friends Reunited
c) ____
d) band at school. Geoff was the
e) ____
f) the drums. They wrote a
g) ____
h) do before we're 30'. Darren asks
i) ____
j) ring so they can arrange to meet.

- When was the last time you got in touch with an old friend? Tell your partner.

16 dotcom

Page 69. Close up. Present perfect, 4

You are going to talk to your partner about things you've both done.

- Complete the *Me* column to make the sentences true for you. Add one sentence of your own.
- Ask your partner questions beginning: *What's the ...?* and complete the *My partner* column.
  For example: *B: What's the best computer game you've ever played? A: Er, Tomb Raider. It's fantastic.*
- Discuss your answers.

Me	My partner
a) The best computer game I've ever played is ____ .	The best computer game he/she's ever played is ____ .
b) The best film I've ever seen is ____ .	____
c) The best live concert I've ever been to is ____ .	____
d) The best-looking man I've ever seen is ____ .	____
e) The strangest food I've ever eaten is ____ .	____
f) The most beautiful place I've ever been to is ____ .	____
g) ____	____

17 Drive

Page 71. Close up. Questions with *How* + adverb/adjective & *What* + noun, 3

You are going to ask questions and compare information about you and your partner.

- Read the *Who* questions in column A, and complete the *How* and *What* questions in column B which will give you the information you want about you and your partner.
- Ask your partner the questions in column B and ⟨circle⟩ the appropriate answer (*Me* or *My partner*) in column A.
- Compare your answers with other students. Find out the answer to each question in column A for the class.

A: Who ...? – Me or my partner?	B
a) Who travels by bus the most? (*Me/My partner*)	How often *do you travel by bus*?
b) Who starts work the earliest? (*Me/My partner*)	What time ____?
c) Who has the oldest car? (*Me/My partner*)	How old ____?
d) Who can get the most people in their car? (*Me/My partner*)	How many ____?
e) Who lives the furthest from the town centre? (*Me/My partner*)	How far ____?
f) Who takes the longest to get ready in the morning? (*Me/My partner*)	How long ____?

18 Justice

Page 76. Punctuation, 2

You have some lines of the story, *Usher's revenge*, and Student A has the other lines.

- Take it in turns to dictate your lines to each other including punctuation and capital letters.
- Complete and then compare your stories. They should be identical.
- What was the usher's revenge?

Usher's revenge

A: ____
B: to see a mystery play,
A: ____
B: from the stage.
A: ____
B: "Find me a better seat
A: ____
B: The usher moved him into the front row
A: ____
B: The usher looked at his tip for a moment
A: ____
B: "The wife did it!"

Wordlist

Abbreviations

n: noun
v: verb
adj: adjective
adv: adverb
num: number
ques: question word
sb: somebody
sth: something
C: countable
U: uncountable
npl: noun plural
★★★: the most common and basic words
★★: very common words
★: fairly common words

Unit 0

act (sth out) *v* /ækt/ ★★★
answer *n C* /'ɑːnsə/ ★★★
article *n C* /'ɑːtɪk(ə)l/ ★★★
bag *n C* /bæg/ ★★★
board *n C* /bɔːd/ ★★★
book *n C* /bʊk/ ★★★
cassette *n C* /kə'set/
cassette player *n C* /kə'set pleɪə/
chair *n C* /tʃeə/ ★★★
check *v* /tʃek/ ★★★
classroom *n C* /'klɑːsruːm/ ★★
conversation *n C* /kɒnvə'seɪʃ(ə)n/ ★★★
correct *adj* /kə'rekt/ ★★★
definition *n C* /defɪ'nɪʃ(ə)n/ ★★
desk *n C* /desk/ ★★★
dictionary (-ies) *n C* /'dɪkʃən(ə)ri/
door *n C* /dɔː/ ★★★
example *n C* /ɪg'zɑːmp(ə)l/ ★★★
– for example /fə(r) ɪg'zɑːmp(ə)l/
group *n C* /gruːp/ ★★★
how *ques* /haʊ/ ★★★
instruction *n C* /ɪn'strʌkʃ(ə)n/ ★★★
listen (to sb/sth) *v* /'lɪs(ə)n/ ★★★
look (at sb/sth) *v* /lʊk/ ★★★
map *n C* /mæp/ ★★
match (with sb/sth) *v* /mætʃ/ ★★
mean (meant, meant) *v* /miːn/ ★★★
– What does ... mean? /wɒt dəz ... 'miːn/
order *n C* /'ɔːdə/ ★★★
– in the correct order /ɪn ðə kərekt 'ɔːdə/
paper *n U* /'peɪpə/ ★★★
partner *n C* /'pɑːtnə/ ★★★
pen *n C* /pen/ ★★
photograph *n C* /'fəʊtəgrɑːf/ ★★★
picture *n C* /'pɪktʃə/ ★★★
piece (-s) of paper *n C* /piːs əv 'peɪpə/

point (to sb/sth) *v* /pɔɪnt/ ★★★
practise *v* /'præktɪs/ ★★
question *n C* /'kwestʃ(ə)n/ ★★★
read (read, read) *v* /riːd/ ★★★
repeat *v* /rɪ'piːt/ ★★★
– Can you repeat that? /kən juː rɪ'piːt ðæt/
say (said, said) *v* /seɪ/ ★★★
– How do you say ... in English?
  /haʊ duː juː seɪ ... in 'ɪŋglɪʃ/
sentence *n C* /'sentəns/ ★★★
song *n C* /sɒŋ/ ★★★
spell (spelt/spelled, spelt/spelled) *v* /spel/ ★
– How do you spell ...? /haʊ duː juː spel .../
student *n C* /'stjuːdənt/ ★★★
teacher *n C* /'tiːtʃə/ ★★★
text *n C* /tekst/ ★★★
thing *n C* /θɪŋ/ ★★★
translate *v* /trænz'leɪt/ ★
underlined *adj* /ʌndə'laɪnd/
understand (understood, understood) *v*
  /ʌndə'stænd/ ★★★
– I don't understand. /aɪ dəʊnt ʌndə'stænd/
use *v* /juːz/ ★★★
window *n C* /'wɪndəʊ/ ★★★
word *n C* /wɜːd/ ★★★
work (with sb/sth) *v* /wɜːk/ ★★★

Unit 1

abbreviation *n C* /əbriːvi'eɪʃ(ə)n/
actor *n C* /'æktə/ ★★★
address *n C* /ə'dres/ ★★★
afternoon *n C* /ɑːftə'nuːn/ ★★★
– Good afternoon. /gʊd ɑːftə'nuːn/
age *n C* /eɪdʒ/ ★★★
alphabet *n C* /'ælfəbet/ ★
angry *adj* /'æŋgri/ ★★★
ask *v* /ɑːsk/ ★★★
ask a question /ɑːsk ə 'kwestʃ(ə)n/
beer *n U* /bɪə/ ★
bicycle *n C* /'baɪsɪk(ə)l/
bike *n C* /baɪk/ ★★★
box (-es) *n C* /bɒks/ ★★★
brother *n C* /'brʌðə/ ★★★
car *n C* /kɑː/ ★★★
category (-ies) *n C* /'kætəg(ə)ri/
certainly *adv* /'sɜːtənli/ ★★★
choose (chose, chosen) *v* /tʃuːz/ ★★★
city (-ies) *n C* /'sɪti/ ★★★
class (-es) *n C* /klɑːs/ ★★★
class ring *n C* /klɑːs 'rɪŋ/
club *n C* /klʌb/ ★★★
coffee *n U* /'kɒfi/ ★★★
colour *n C* /'kʌlə/ ★★★

Colours

black *adj* /blæk/ ★★★
blue *adj* /bluː/ ★
green *adj* /griːn/ ★★★
grey *adj* /greɪ/ ★
red *adj* /red/ ★★★
white *adj* /waɪt/ ★
yellow *adj* /'jeləʊ/ ★★★

company (-ies) *n C* /'kʌmpəni/ ★★★
complete *v* /kəm'pliːt/ ★★★
computer *n C* /kəm'pjuːtə/ ★★★
copy (copied, copied) *v* /'kɒpi/ ★★★
dancing *n U* /'dɑːnsɪŋ/
day *n C* /deɪ/ ★★★

Days of the week

Monday *n U* /'mʌndeɪ/ ★★★
Tuesday *n U* /'tjuːzdeɪ/ ★★★
Wednesday *n U* /'wenzdeɪ/ ★★★
Thursday *n U* /'θɜːzdeɪ/ ★★★
Friday *n U* /'fraɪdeɪ/ ★★★
Saturday *n U* /'sætədeɪ/ ★★★
Sunday *n U* /'sʌndeɪ/ ★★★

dictate *v* /dɪk'teɪt/
different *adj* /'dɪfrənt/ ★★★
discuss *v* /dɪs'kʌs/ ★★★
double (+ letter/number) *adj* /'dʌb(ə)l/ ★★
drink *n C* /drɪŋk/ ★★★
drive (drove, driven) *v* /draɪv/ ★★★
engineer *n C* /endʒɪ'nɪə/ ★
favourite *adj* /'feɪv(ə)rɪt/ ★★
first name *n C* /'fɜːst neɪm/
food *n U* /fuːd/ ★★★
golf club *n C* /'gɒlf klʌb/
gym *n C* /dʒɪm/
hamburger *n C* /'hæmbɜːgə/
happy *adj* /'hæpi/ ★★★
health *n U* /helθ/ ★★★
hear (heard, heard) *v* /hɪə/ ★★★
help *v* /help/ ★★★
– Can I help you? /kən aɪ 'help juː/
holiday *n C* /'hɒlɪdeɪ/ ★★★
hungry *adj* /'hʌŋgri/ ★
information *n U* /ɪnfə'meɪʃ(ə)n/ ★★★
interest *n C* /'ɪntrəst/ ★★★
interested (in) *adj* /'ɪntrəstɪd/ ★★★
interview *v* /'ɪntəvjuː/ ★
join *v* /dʒɔɪn/ ★★★
karaoke *n U* /kæri'əʊki/
know (knew, known) (about sb/sth) *v*
  /nəʊ/ ★★★
– I don't know. /aɪ dəʊnt 'nəʊ/
label (labelled, labelled) *v* /'leɪb(ə)l/

language *n C* /ˈlæŋgwɪdʒ/ ★★★
letter *n C* /ˈletə/ ★★★
like *v* /laɪk/ ★★★
– **I'd like to …** /aɪd ˈlaɪk tə…/
live *v* /lɪv/ ★★★
love *n U* /lʌv/ ★★★
man (men) *n C* /mæn/ ★★★
marital status *n U* /ˈmærɪt(ə)l steɪtəs/
married *adj* /ˈmærɪd/ ★★★
maybe *adv* /ˈmeɪbi/ ★★★
meaning *n C* /ˈmiːnɪŋ/ ★★★
member *n C* /ˈmembə/ ★★★
memory (-ies) *n C* /ˈmem(ə)ri/ ★★★
mobile phone *n C* /ˈməʊbaɪl ˈfəʊn/
month *n C* /mʌnθ/ ★★★

Months of the year

January *n U* /ˈdʒænjʊəri/ ★★★
February *n U* /ˈfebrʊəri/ ★★★
March *n U* /mɑːtʃ/ ★★★
April *n U* /ˈeɪprəl/ ★★★
May *n U* /meɪ/ ★★★
June *n U* /dʒuːn/ ★★★
July *n U* /dʒʊˈlaɪ/ ★★★
August *n U* /ˈɔːgəst/ ★★★
September *n U* /sepˈtembə/ ★★★
October *n U* /ɒkˈtəʊbə/ ★★★
November *n U* /nəʊˈvembə/ ★★★
December *n U* /dɪˈsembə/ ★★★

motorbike *n C* /ˈməʊtəbaɪk/
name *n C* /neɪm/ ★★★
near *prep* /nɪə/ ★★★
near here /nɪə ˈhɪə/
nervous *adj* /ˈnɜːvəs/ ★★
number *n C* /ˈnʌmbə/ ★★★
occupation *n C* /ɒkjəˈpeɪʃ(ə)n/ ★
old *adj* /əʊld/ ★★★
pasta *n U* /ˈpæstə/
penknife (-ves) *n C* /ˈpennaɪf/
pet *n C* /pet/ ★
phone number *n C* /ˈfəʊn nʌmbə/
pronunciation *n C* /prənʌnsiˈeɪʃ(ə)n/ ★
record *n C* /ˈrekɔːd/
recording *n C* /rɪˈkɔːdɪŋ/
ring *n C* /rɪŋ/ ★★★
sad *adj* /sæd/ ★★
sea *n U* /siː/ ★★★
see (saw, seen) *v* /siː/ ★★★
singer *n C* /ˈsɪŋə/
single *adj* /ˈsɪŋg(ə)l/ ★★★
sister *n C* /ˈsɪstə/ ★★★
smoke *v* /sməʊk/ ★★
sound *n C* /saʊnd/ ★★★
speak (spoke, spoken) *v* /spiːk/ ★★★
spelling *n C* /ˈspelɪŋ/

sport *n C* /spɔːt/ ★★★

Sports

aerobics *npl* /eəˈrəʊbɪks/
basketball *n U* /ˈbɑːskɪtbɔːl/
boxing *n U* /ˈbɒksɪŋ/
football *n U* /ˈfʊtbɔːl/ ★★
golf *n U* /gɒlf/ ★
skiing *n U* /ˈskiːɪŋ/
squash *n U* /skwɒʃ/
swimming *n U* /ˈswɪmɪŋ/
tennis *n U* /ˈtenɪs/

stressed *adj* /strest/
summer holiday *n C* /ˈsʌmə ˈhɒlɪdeɪ/
surname *n C* /ˈsɜːneɪm/
sushi *n U* /ˈsuːʃi/
table *n C* /ˈteɪbl/ ★★★
tai chi *n U* /taɪ ˈtʃiː/
take (took, taken) *v* /teɪk/ ★★★
take it in turns to … /teɪk ɪt ɪn ˈtɜːnz tə/
task *n C* /tɑːsk/ ★★★
tea *n U* /tiː/ ★★★
telephone number *n C* /ˈteləfəʊn nʌmbə/
television *n C* /ˈteləvɪʒn/ ★★★
think (of) (thought, thought) *v* /θɪŋk/ ★★★
tired *adj* /ˈtaɪəd/ ★★★
travel *n U* /ˈtræv(ə)l/ ★★★
true *adj* /truː/ ★★★
underline *v* /ʌndəˈlaɪn/
useful *adj* /ˈjuːsfʊl/ ★★★
want *v* /wɒnt/ ★★★
watch *v* /wɒtʃ/ ★★★
watch television /wɒtʃ ˈteləvɪʒ(ə)n/
water *n U* /ˈwɔːtə/ ★★★
week *n C* /wiːk/ ★★★
what *ques* /wɒt/ ★★★
where *ques* /weə/ ★★★
woman (women) *n C* /ˈwʊmən/ ★★★
work (for) *v* /wɜːk/ ★★★
write (sth down) (wrote, written) *v* /raɪt/ ★★★
writer *n C* /ˈraɪtə/ ★★★
year *n C* /jɪə/ ★★★
yoga *n U* /ˈjəʊgə/

Unit 2

bedroom *n C* /ˈbedruːm/ ★★
boyfriend *n C* /ˈbɔɪfrend/ ★
centre *n C* /ˈsentə/ ★★★
cider *n U* /ˈsaɪdə/
city (-ies) *n C* /ˈsɪti/ ★★★
city centre *n C* /sɪti ˈsentə/

country (-ies) *n C* /ˈkʌntri/ ★★★

Countries

Argentina *n C* /ɑːdʒənˈtiːnə/
Brazil *n C* /brəˈzɪl/
France *n C* /frɑːns/
Germany *n C* /ˈdʒɜːməni/
Italy *n C* /ˈɪtəli/
Japan *n C* /dʒəˈpæn/
Poland *n C* /ˈpəʊlənd/
Spain *n C* /speɪn/
United Kingdom *n C* /juːnaɪtɪd ˈkɪŋdəm/
USA *n C* /juː es ˈeɪ/

describe *v* /dɪsˈkraɪb/ ★★★
description *n C* /dɪsˈkrɪpʃ(ə)n/ ★★★
DJ *n C* /ˈdiː dʒeɪ/
doctor *n C* /ˈdɒktə/ ★★★
family (-ies) *n C* /ˈfæm(ə)li/ ★★★

Family words

aunt *n C* /ɑːnt/ ★★
baby (-ies) *n C* /ˈbeɪbi/ ★★★
child (children) *n C* /tʃaɪld/ ★★★
couple *n C* /ˈkʌp(ə)l/ ★★★
cousin *n C* /ˈkʌz(ə)n/ ★★
daughter *n C* /ˈdɔːtə/ ★★★
father *n C* /ˈfɑːðə/ ★★★
grandfather *n C* /ˈgræn(d)fɑːðə/ ★
grandmother *n C* /ˈgræn(d)mʌðə/ ★
mother *n C* /ˈmʌðə/ ★★★
nephew *n C* /ˈnefjuː/
niece *n C* /niːs/
parent *n C* /ˈpeərənt/ ★★★
relative *n C* /ˈrelətɪv/ ★
sister(-s)-in-law *n C* /ˈsɪstə(r)ɪnlɔː/
son *n C* /sʌn/ ★★★
uncle *n C* /ˈʌŋk(ə)l/ ★

family tree *n C* /ˈfæm(ə)li ˈtriː/
girlfriend *n C* /ˈgɜːlfrend/ ★
hospital *n C* /ˈhɒspɪt(ə)l/ ★★★
interesting *adj* /ˈɪntrəstɪŋ/ ★★★
international *adj* /ɪntəˈnæʃn(ə)l/ ★★★
job *n C* /dʒɒb/ ★★★

Languages

English *n* /ˈɪŋglɪʃ/
French *n* /frentʃ/
German *n* /ˈdʒɜːmən/
Italian *n* /ɪˈtæliən/
Japanese *n* /dʒæpəˈniːz/
Polish *n* /ˈpəʊlɪʃ/
Portuguese *n* /pɔːtʃʊˈgiːz/
Spanish *n* /ˈspænɪʃ/

live next door to … /lɪv neks(t) ˈdɔː tə/
lovely *adj* /ˈlʌvli/
mechanic *n C* /məˈkænɪk/
meet (met, met) *v* /miːt/ ★★★

nationality (-ies) n C /ˌnæʃ(ə)ˈnælɪti/ ★

nice adj /naɪs/ ★★★
night club n C /ˈnaɪt klʌb/
nurse n C /nɜːs/ ★★
office n C /ˈɒfɪs/ ★★★
part-time job n C /ˌpɑːttaɪm ˈdʒɒb/
person (people) n C /ˈpɜːs(ə)n/ ★★★
piano n C /piˈænəʊ/ ★
play v /pleɪ/ ★★★
play the piano /pleɪ ðə piˈænəʊ/
relation n C /rɪˈleɪʃ(ə)n/ ★★★
restaurant n C /ˈrest(ə)rɒnt/ ★★★
retired adj /rɪˈtaɪəd/
sales manager n C /ˈseɪlz mænɪdʒə/
school n C /skuːl/ ★★★
secretary (-ies) n C /ˈsekrət(ə)ri/ ★
talk (about sth) v /tɔːk/ ★★★
twin adj /twɪn/
university (-ies) n C /ˌjuːnɪˈvɜːsɪti/ ★★★
waiter n C /ˈweɪtə/

Unit 3

activity (-ies) n C /ækˈtɪvɪti/ ★★★

alcohol n U /ˈælkəhɒl/ ★
bed n C /bed/ ★★★
bird n C /bɜːd/ ★★★
birthday n C /ˈbɜːθdeɪ/ ★★
boss (-es) n C /bɒs/ ★★
breakfast n U /ˈbrekfəst/ ★★
camping n U /ˈkæmpɪŋ/
card n C /kɑːd/ ★★★
cat n C /kæt/ ★★★
chocolate n U /ˈtʃɒk(ə)lət/ ★★
Christmas n C /ˈkrɪsməs/ ★★★
clubbing n U /ˈklʌbɪŋ/
computer game n C /kəmˈpjuːtə geɪm/

compare v /kəmˈpeə/ ★★★
concert n C /ˈkɒnsət/ ★★
cry (cried, cried) v /kraɪ/ ★★★
daily adj /ˈdeɪli/ ★★
dinner n U /ˈdɪnə/ ★★★
do (did, done) v /duː/ ★★★

dream n C /driːm/ ★★★
early adv /ˈɜːli/ ★★★
Easter n C /ˈiːstə/
eating out n U /iːtɪŋ ˈaʊt/
evening n C /ˈiːvnɪŋ/ ★★★
film n C /fɪlm/ ★★★
finish v /ˈfɪnɪʃ/ ★★★
fish (fish) n C/U /fɪʃ/ ★★★
friend n C /frend/ ★★★
game n C /geɪm/ ★★★
get (got, got) v /get/ ★★★
get up late /get ʌp ˈleɪt/
give (gave, given) v /gɪv/ ★★★
go (went, been/gone) v /gəʊ/ ★★★

hate v /heɪt/ ★★★
have (had, had) v /hæv/ ★★★

hour n C /ˈaʊə/ ★★★
housework n U /ˈhaʊswɜːk/
ironing n U /ˈaɪənɪŋ/
jazz n U /dʒæz/
jogging n U /ˈdʒɒgɪŋ/
large adj /lɑːdʒ/ ★★★
laugh v /lɑːf/ ★★★
learn (learnt/learned, learnt/learned) v /lɜːn/ ★★★
lesson n C /ˈles(ə)n/ ★★★
light n C /laɪt/ ★★★
little adj /ˈlɪt(ə)l/ ★★★
lose (lost, lost) v /luːz/ ★★★

loud adj /laʊd/ ★★
love v /lʌv/ ★★★
lunch (-es) n U /lʌntʃ/ ★★★
make (made, made) v /meɪk/ ★★★

meat n U /miːt/ ★★★
midnight n C /ˈmɪdnaɪt/ ★
mind v /maɪnd/ ★★★
– I don't mind ... /aɪ dəʊnt ˈmaɪnd/
model n C /ˈmɒd(ə)l/ ★★★
morning n C /ˈmɔːnɪŋ/ ★★★
music n U /ˈmjuːzɪk/ ★★★
nap n C /næp/
need v /niːd/ ★★★
newspaper n C /ˈnjuːspeɪpə/ ★★★
night n C /naɪt/ ★★★
open adj /ˈəʊp(ə)n/ ★★★
outside adv /aʊtˈsaɪd/ ★★★
park n C /pɑːk/ ★★
party n C /ˈpɑːti/ ★★★
pay (paid, paid) v /peɪ/ ★★★
perfect adj /ˈpɜːfɪkt/ ★★
present n C /ˈprez(ə)nt/ ★★★
pyjamas npl /pɪˈdʒɑːməz/
radio n C /ˈreɪdiəʊ/ ★★★
really adv /ˈrɪəli/ ★★★
reggae n U /ˈregeɪ/
remember v /rɪˈmembə/ ★★★
roast dinner n C /rəʊst ˈdɪnə/
rock concert n C /ˈrɒk kɒnsət/
shopping n U /ˈʃɒpɪŋ/ ★★
shower n C /ˈʃaʊə/ ★
similar (to) adj /ˈsɪmɪlə/ ★★★
sleep (slept, slept) v /sliːp/ ★★★
spend (spent, spent) v /spend/ ★★★
start v /stɑːt/ ★★★
stay (in) v /steɪ/ ★★★
summer n C /ˈsʌmə/ ★★★
sumo wrestler n C /ˈsuːməʊ ˈreslə/
teach (taught, taught) v /tiːtʃ/ ★★★
train v /treɪn/ ★★★
vegetable n C /ˈvedʒtəb(ə)l/ ★★★
video n C /ˈvɪdiəʊ/ ★★★
video game n C /ˈvɪdiəʊ geɪm/
walk n C /wɔːk/ ★★
want v /wɒnt/ ★★★
washing up n U /wɒʃɪŋ ˈʌp/
watch v /wɒtʃ/ ★★★
weekend n C /wiːkˈend/ ★★★
win (won, won) v /wɪn/ ★★★
window n C /ˈwɪndəʊ/ ★★★
winter n C /ˈwɪntə/ ★★★

Unit 4

armchair *n C* /ˈɑːmtʃeə/
awful *adj* /ˈɔːfʊl/ ★★
ballroom *n C* /ˈbɔːlruːm/
bank *n C* /bæŋk/ ★★★
bath *n C* /bɑːθ/ ★★★
beach (-es) *n C* /biːtʃ/ ★★
blind *n C* /blaɪnd/
block (-s) **of flats** *n C* /blɒk əv ˈflæts/
bookcase *n C* /ˈbʊkkeɪs/
carpet *n C* /ˈkɑːpɪt/ ★★
cheap *adj* /tʃiːp/ ★★★
clean *adj* /kliːn/ ★★★
clock *n C* /klɒk/ ★★★
coffee table *n C* /ˈkɒfi: teɪb(ə)l/
cold *adj* /kəʊld/ ★★★
cooker *n C* /ˈkʊkə/
corner *n C* /ˈkɔːnə/ ★★★
cupboard *n C* /ˈkʌbəd/ ★
curtain *n C* /ˈkɜːt(ə)n/ ★★★
cushion *n C* /ˈkʊʃ(ə)n/
dark *adj* /dɑːk/ ★★★
delicious *adj* /dɪˈlɪʃ(ə)s/ ★
dirty *adj* /ˈdɜːti/ ★★★
dishwasher *n C* /ˈdɪʃwɒʃə/
dry *adj* /draɪ/ ★★★
expensive *adj* /ɪkˈspensɪv/ ★★★
fan *n C* /fæn/ ★★
festival *n C* /ˈfestɪv(ə)l/
fireplace *n C* /ˈfaɪəpleɪs/
flat *n C* /flæt/ ★★
floor *n C* /flɔː/ ★★★
fridge *n C* /frɪdʒ/ ★
friendly *adj* /ˈfrendli/ ★★
furniture *n U* /ˈfɜːnɪtʃə/ ★★
guest *n C* /gest/ ★★
hill *n C* /hɪl/ ★★★
home *n C* /həʊm/ ★★★
horoscope *n C* /ˈhɒrəskəʊp/
horrible *adj* /ˈhɒrɪb(ə)l/ ★
hotel *n C* /həʊˈtel/ ★★★
house *n C* /haʊs/ ★★★
indoor swimming pool *n C*
  /ɪndɔː ˈswɪmɪŋ puːl/
island *n C* /ˈaɪlənd/ ★★★
lake *n C* /leɪk/ ★★
lamp *n C* /læmp/ ★★
light *adj* /laɪt/ ★★★
magazine *n C* /mægəˈziːn/ ★★
mirror *n C* /ˈmɪrə/ ★★
miserable *adj* /ˈmɪz(ə)rəb(ə)l/
modern *adj* /ˈmɒd(ə)n/ ★★★
money *n U* /ˈmʌni/ ★★★
mountain *n C* /ˈmaʊntɪn/ ★★★
museum *n C* /mjuːˈziːəm/ ★★★
painting *n C* /ˈpeɪntɪŋ/ ★★
palace *n C* /ˈpælɪs/
plant *n C* /plɑːnt/ ★★★
poster *n C* /ˈpəʊstə/

Prepositions of place

above *prep* /əˈbʌv/ ★★★
by *prep* /baɪ/ ★★★
in *prep* /ɪn/ ★★★
in front of *prep* /ɪn ˈfrʌnt əv/
near *prep* /ˈnɪə/ ★★★
next to *prep* /neks(t) tə/
on *prep* /ɒn/ ★★★
under *prep* /ˈʌndə/ ★★★

press *n U* /pres/ ★★★
print *n C* /prɪnt/ ★
radiator *n C* /ˈreɪdieɪtə/
reception *n C* /rɪˈsepʃ(ə)n/ ★
recording studio *n C* /rɪˈkɔːdɪŋ stjuːdiəʊ/
river *n C* /ˈrɪvə/ ★★★
room *n C* /ruːm/ ★★★

Rooms

bathroom *n C* /ˈbɑːθruːm/ ★★
bedroom *n C* /ˈbedruːm/ ★★
kitchen *n C* /ˈkɪtʃɪn/ ★★★
living room *n C* /ˈlɪvɪŋ ruːm/
playroom *n C* /ˈpleɪruːm/

royal *adj* /ˈrɔɪəl/ ★★
rug *n C* /rʌg/
ruin *n C* /ˈruːɪn/
shelf (-ves) *n C* /ʃelf/ ★★
shop *n C* /ʃɒp/ ★★★
shower *n C* /ˈʃaʊə/ ★
sign *n C* /saɪn/ ★★★
sink *n C* /sɪŋk/ ★★
sofa *n C* /ˈsəʊfə/
star *n C* /stɑː/ ★★★
star sign *n C* /ˈstɑː saɪn/
stereo *n C* /ˈsteriəʊ/
street *n C* /striːt/ ★★★
swimming pool *n C* /ˈswɪmɪŋ puːl/
television *n C* /teləˈvɪʒ(ə)n/ ★★★
terrible *adj* /ˈterɪb(ə)l/ ★★
throne *n C* /θrəʊn/
tidy *adj* /ˈtaɪdi/ ★
toilet *n C* /ˈtɔɪlət/ ★
top floor *n C* /tɒp ˈflɔː/
tourist *n C* /ˈtʊərɪst/ ★★
unfriendly *adj* /ʌnˈfrendli/
village *n C* /ˈvɪlɪdʒ/ ★★★
visit *v* /ˈvɪzɪt/ ★★★
wardrobe *n C* /ˈwɔːdrəʊb/
warm *adj* /wɔːm/ ★★★
washbasin *n C* /ˈwɒʃbeɪs(ə)n/
washing machine *n C* /ˈwɒʃɪŋ məʃiːn/
weather *n U* /ˈweðə/ ★★★
wedding *n C* /ˈwedɪŋ/ ★★
wet *adj* /wet/ ★★★
wonderful *adj* /ˈwʌndəfʊl/ ★★

Unit 5

church *n C* /tʃɜːtʃ/ ★★★
college *n C* /ˈkɒlɪdʒ/ ★★★
courier *n C* /ˈkʊriə/
flower *n C* /ˈflaʊə/ ★★★
foreign *adj* /ˈfɒrən/ ★★★
full-time job *n C* /fʊl taɪm ˈdʒɒb/
homestay *adj* /ˈhəʊmsteɪ/
poetry *n U* /ˈpəʊətri/ ★
shorts *npl* /ʃɔːts/
sweet *adj* /swiːt/ ★★

Unit 6

bar *n C* /bɑː/ ★★★
base (sth on) *v* /beɪs/ ★★★
bowl *n C* /bəʊl/ ★★
bread *n U* /bred/ ★★★
cake *n C* /keɪk/ ★★
calorie *n C* /ˈkæləri/
carbohydrate *n C/U* /kɑːbəˈhaɪdreɪt/
cereal *n C* /ˈsɪəriəl/
cheese *n U* /tʃiːz/ ★★
chicken *n U* /ˈtʃɪkɪn/ ★★
chips *npl* /tʃɪps/
container *n C* /kənˈteɪnə/ ★★

Containers

bottle *n C* /ˈbɒt(ə)l/ ★★★
can *n C* /kæn/ ★★
carton *n C* /ˈkɑːt(ə)n/
jar *n C* /dʒɑː/
packet *n C* /ˈpækɪt/ ★
tin *n C* /tɪn/ ★
tub *n C* /tʌb/

dessert *n U* /dɪˈzɜːt/ ★
diet *n C* /ˈdaɪət/ ★★
digest *v* /daɪˈdʒest/
diva *n C* /ˈdiːvə/
DVD *n C* /diː viː ˈdiː/
egg *n C* /eg/ ★★★
fruit *n U* /fruːt/ ★★★

Fruit

apple *n C* /ˈæp(ə)l/ ★★★
banana *n C* /bəˈnɑːnə/
melon *n C* /ˈmelən/
grape *n C* /greɪp/
lemon *n C* /ˈlemən/
orange *n C* /ˈɒrɪndʒ/ ★★
pear *n C* /peə/
strawberry (-ies) *n C* /ˈstrɔːb(ə)ri/

fruit salad *n U* /fruːt ˈsæləd/
healthy *adj* /ˈhelθi/ ★★
item *n C* /ˈaɪtəm/ ★★★
jewellery *n U* /ˈdʒuːəlri/ ★★
kitten *n C* /ˈkɪt(ə)n/

meal *n C* /miːl/ ★★★
menu *n C* /ˈmenjuː/ ★
olive oil *n U* /ˈɒlɪv ˈɔɪl/
protein *n C/U* /ˈprəʊtiːn/
puppy (-ies) *n C* /ˈpʌpi/
research *n U* /ˈriːsɜːtʃ, rɪˈsɜːtʃ/ ★★
rice *n U* /raɪs/ ★
sandwich (-es) *n C* /ˈsæn(d)wɪdʒ/ ★
seafood *n U* /ˈsiːfuːd/
slim *adj* /slɪm/ ★★
spaghetti bolognese *n U* /spəˈgeti bɒləˈneɪz/
steak *n U* /steɪk/
tomato (-es) *n C* /təˈmɑːtəʊ/
unhealthy *adj* /ʌnˈhelθi/
vase *n C* /vɑːz/

Vegetables

bean *n C* /biːn/
carrot *n C* /ˈkærət/
cauliflower *n C* /ˈkɒlɪflaʊə/
garlic *n U* /ˈgɑːlɪk/
mushroom *n C* /ˈmʌʃruːm/
onion *n C* /ˈʌnjən/
pepper *n C* /ˈpepə/
potato (-es) *n C* /pəˈteɪtəʊ/ ★★

Unit 7

application *n C* /æplɪˈkeɪʃ(ə)n/ ★★
baggy *adj* /ˈbægi/
career *n C* /kəˈrɪə/ ★★
character *n C* /ˈkærɪktə/ ★★★

Words to describe character

adventurous *adj* /ədˈventʃərəs/
ambitious *adj* /æmˈbɪʃəs/
artistic *adj* /ɑːˈtɪstɪk/
cheerful *adj* /ˈtʃɪəf(ə)l/
clever *adj* /ˈklevə/ ★★
confident *adj* /ˈkɒnfɪdənt/ ★★★
creative *adj* /kriːˈeɪtɪv/ ★
easy-going *adj* /ˈiːzɪgəʊɪŋ/
energetic *adj* /enəˈdʒetɪk/
hard-working *adj* /ˈhɑːdwɜːkɪŋ/
helpful *adj* /ˈhelpfʊl/
honest *adj* /ˈɒnɪst/ ★
independent *adj* /ɪndəˈpendənt/ ★★★
kind *adj* /kaɪnd/ ★★★
practical *adj* /ˈpræktɪk(ə)l/ ★★★
romantic *adj* /rəʊˈmæntɪk/
sensible *adj* /ˈsensɪb(ə)l/ ★
sensitive *adj* /ˈsensɪtɪv/
serious *adj* /ˈsɪəriəs/ ★★★
shy *adj* /ʃaɪ/ ★
sociable *adj* /ˈsəʊʃəb(ə)l/
strong *adj* /strɒŋ/ ★★★

---

clean *adj* /kliːn/ ★★★
clothes *npl* /kləʊðz/ ★★★
crash helmet *n C* /ˈkræʃ helmɪt/
designer clothes *npl* /dɪzaɪnə ˈkləʊðz/
earn *v* /ɜːn/ ★★
exam *n C* /ɪgˈzæm/ ★★
fail *v* /feɪl/ ★★★
famous *adj* /ˈfeɪməs/ ★★★
fattening *adj* /ˈfæt(ə)nɪŋ/
formal *adj* /ˈfɔːm(ə)l/ ★★★
good (at) *adj* /gʊd/ ★★★
good-looking *adj* /ˈgʊdlʊkɪŋ/
job *n C* /dʒɒb/ ★★★

Jobs

accountant *n C* /əˈkaʊntənt/
computer programmer *n C*
  /kəmpjuːtə ˈprəʊgræmə/
cook *n C* /kʊk/ ★★★
dancer *n C* /ˈdɑːnsə/
farmer *n C* /ˈfɑːmə/
graphic designer *n C* /græfɪk dɪˈzaɪnə/
lawyer *n C* /ˈlɔːjə/ ★★
musician *n C* /mjuːˈzɪʃ(ə)n/ ★
politician *n C* /pɒlɪˈtɪʃ(ə)n/ ★★
sales assistant *n C* /ˈseɪlz əsɪstənt/
scientist *n C* /ˈsaɪəntɪst/ ★★
secondary school teacher *n C*
  /ˈsekənd(ə)ri skuːl ˈtiːtʃə/
security guard *n C* /sɪˈkjʊərəti gɑːd/
shop assistant *n C* /ˈʃɒp əsɪstənt/
snowboarder *n C* /ˈsnəʊbɔːdə/
sports instructor *n C* /ˈspɔːts ɪnstrʌktə/
tourist guide *n C* /ˈtʊərɪst gaɪd/
tour leader *n C* /ˈtʊə liːdə/

---

letter of application *n C*
  /letə(r) əv æplɪˈkeɪʃ(ə)n/
modelling *n U* /ˈmɒd(ə)lɪŋ/
muscle *n C* /ˈmʌs(ə)l/ ★★
necessary *adj* /ˈnesəs(ə)ri/ ★★★
possible *adj* /ˈpɒsɪb(ə)l/ ★★★
rich *adj* /rɪtʃ/ ★★★
salary (-ies) *n C* /ˈsæləri/ ★
sporty *adj* /ˈspɔːti/
travel (travelled, travelled) *v* /ˈtræv(ə)l/ ★★★

Unit 8

ago *adv* /əˈgəʊ/ ★★★
at first *adv* /ət ˈfɜːst/
attack *n C* /əˈtæk/ ★★★
bingo *n U* /ˈbɪŋgəʊ/
boat *n C* /bəʊt/ ★★★
book *v* /bʊk/ ★
brand *n C* /brænd/ ★
climate *n C* /ˈklaɪmət/ ★★
credit card *n C* /ˈkredɪt kɑːd/
dolphin *n C* /ˈdɒlfɪn/
eventually *adv* /ɪˈventʃʊ(ə)li/ ★★★
flight *n C* /flaɪt/ ★★★
foreigner *n C* /ˈfɒrɪnə/

---

go fishing /gəʊ ˈfɪʃɪŋ/
haircut *n C* /ˈheəkʌt/
have a haircut /hæv ə ˈheəkʌt/
hero (-es) *n C* /ˈhɪərəʊ/
inside *adv* /ɪnˈsaɪd/ ★★★
one day *adv* /wʌn ˈdeɪ/
pirate *n C* /ˈpaɪrət/
shark *n C* /ˈʃɑːk/
sportswear *n U* /ˈspɔːtsweə/
suddenly *adv* /ˈsʌd(ə)nli/ ★★★
tent *n C* /tent/
take a photograph (of sb/sth)
  /teɪk ə ˈfəʊtəgrɑːf/
water sport *n C* /ˈwɔːtə spɔːt/

Water sports

canoeing *n U* /kəˈnuːɪŋ/
fishing *n U* /ˈfɪʃɪŋ/
kite-surfing *n U* /kaɪt sɜːfɪŋ/
rowing *n U* /ˈrəʊɪŋ/
sailing *n U* /ˈseɪlɪŋ/
scuba-diving *n U* /ˈskuːbə daɪvɪŋ/
surfing *n U* /ˈsɜːfɪŋ/
water-skiing *n U* /ˈwɔːtəskiːɪŋ/
windsurfing *n U* /ˈwɪn(d)sɜːfɪŋ/

---

wetsuit *n C* /ˈwetsuːt/

Unit 9

alone *adv* /əˈləʊn/ ★★
arrive *v* /əˈraɪv/ ★★★
be born (was, been) *v* /biː ˈbɔːn/ ★★★
bored *adj* /bɔːd/ ★★
change *v* /tʃeɪndʒ/ ★★★
danger *n C* /ˈdeɪndʒə/ ★★★
die *v* /daɪ/ ★★★
do exercise /duː ˈeksəsaɪz/
embarrassed *adj* /ɪmˈbærɪst/ ★
excited *adj* /ɪkˈsaɪtɪd/ ★★
exercise *n U* /ˈeksəsaɪz/ ★★★
experience *n C* /ɪkˈspɪəriəns/ ★★★
fall (fell, fallen) *v* /fɔːl/ ★★★
fall in love (with sb/sth) /fɔɪl ɪn ˈlʌv/
feel (felt, felt) *v* /fiːl/ ★★★
foreign *adj* /ˈfɒrɪn/ ★★★
frightened *adj* /ˈfraɪt(ə)nd/ ★
get (got, got) *v* /get/ ★★★

Some expressions with *get*

get a job /get ə ˈdʒɒb/
get divorced (from) /get dɪˈvɔːst/
get engaged (to) /get ɪŋˈgeɪdʒd/
get married (to) /get ˈmærɪd/

Based on data from the *Macmillan Essential Dictionary*

go (went, been/gone) *v* /gəʊ/ ★★★

More expressions with *go*

go clothes shopping /gəʊ ˈkləʊðz ʃɒpɪŋ/
go on holiday /gəʊ ɒn ˈhɒlɪdeɪ/
go out /gəʊ ˈaʊt/
go to school /gəʊ tə ˈskuːl/
go to the cinema /gəʊ tə ðə ˈsɪnəmə/

---

grow up (grew, grown) *v* /grəʊ ˈʌp/
have (had, had) *v* /hæv/ ★★★

More expressions with *have*

have a bad experience
/hæv ə bæd ɪkˈspɪərɪəns/
have a bath /hæv ə ˈbɑːθ/
have a relationship (with)
/hæv ə rɪˈleɪʃ(ə)nʃɪp wɪð/
have children /hæv ˈtʃɪldrən/

---

late (for sb/sth) *adj* /leɪt/ ★★★
leave (left, left) *v* /liːv/ ★★★
leave school /liːv ˈskuːl/
life (-ves) *n C* /laɪf/ ★★★
lonely *adj* /ˈləʊnli/ ★
miss *v* /mɪs/ ★★★
move *v* /muːv/ ★★★
nervous *adj* /ˈnɜːvəs/ ★★
race *n C* /reɪs/ ★★★
retire *v* /rɪˈtaɪə/ ★★
solo *adj* /ˈsəʊləʊ/
spider *n C* /ˈspaɪdə/
study (studied, studied) *v* /ˈstʌdi/ ★★★
traffic *n U* /ˈtræfɪk/ ★★★
traffic jam *n C* /ˈtræfɪk dʒæm/
TV *n U* /tiː ˈviː/ ★★★
voyage *n C* /ˈvɔɪɪdʒ/
watch TV /wɒtʃ tiː ˈviː/
worried *adj* /ˈwʌrɪd/ ★

Unit 10

become (became, become) *v* /bɪˈkʌm/ ★★★
buy (bought, bought) *v* /baɪ/ ★★★
delicious *adj* /dɪˈlɪʃəs/ ★
email *n C* /ˈiːmeɪl/ ★★★
go skiing /gəʊ ˈskiːɪŋ/
hamster *n C* /ˈhæmstə/
helmet *n C* /ˈhelmɪt/
kill *v* /kɪl/ ★★★
make breakfast /meɪk ˈbrekfəst/
shoot (shot, shot) *v* /ʃuːt/ ★★★
start *v* /stɑːt/ ★★★
survive *v* /səˈvaɪv/ ★★★
vote *v* /vəʊt/ ★★★

Unit 11

accessory (-ies) *n C* /əkˈsesəri/
average *adj* /ˈævərɪdʒ/ ★★
beard *n C* /ˈbɪəd/
beautiful *adj* /ˈbjuːtɪfʊl/ ★★★
blond *adj* /blɒnd/
bracelet *n C* /ˈbreɪslət/
casual *adj* /ˈkæʒʊəl/
chain *n C* /tʃeɪn/

Clothes

belt *n C* /belt/ ★
boot *n C* /buːt/ ★★
coat *n C* /kəʊt/ ★★★
dress (-es) *n C* /dres/ ★★★
footwear *n U* /ˈfʊtweə/
hat *n C* /hæt/ ★★
jacket *n C* /ˈdʒækɪt/ ★★
jeans *npl* /dʒiːnz/ ★★
shirt *n C* /ʃɜːt/ ★★★
shoe *n C* /ʃuː/ ★★★
sock *n C* /sɒk/
suit *n C* /suːt/ ★★
sweater *n C* /ˈswetə/
tie *n C* /taɪ/ ★
top *n C* /tɒp/ ★★★
tracksuit *n C* /ˈtræksuːt/
trainers *npl* /ˈtreɪnəz/
trousers *npl* /ˈtraʊzəz/ ★★
T-shirt *n C* /ˈtiː ʃɜːt/
underpants *npl* /ˈʌndəpænts/
underwear *n U* /ˈʌndəweə/

---

curly *adj* /ˈkɜːli/
dark *adj* /dɑːk/ ★★★
earring *n C* /ˈɪərɪŋ/
eye *n C* /aɪ/ ★★★
face *n C* /feɪs/ ★★★
fair *adj* /feə/ ★★★
fan *n C* /fæn/
get (out of sth) *v* /get/ ★★★
get dressed /get ˈdrest/
glasses *npl* /ˈglɑːsɪz/
hair *n U* /heə/ ★★★
handsome *adj* /ˈhæn(d)səm/ ★★
have a good time /hæv ə gʊd ˈtaɪm/
head *n C* /hed/ ★★★
highlights *npl* /ˈhaɪlaɪts/
hold (held, held) *v* /həʊld/ ★★★
lipstick *n C* /ˈlɪpstɪk/
long *adj* /lɒŋ/ ★★★
look like *v* /ˈlʊk laɪk/
medium-length *adj* /ˈmiːdiəm leŋθ/
moustache *n C* /məsˈtɑːʃ/
pretty *adj* /ˈprɪti/ ★
put (sth on) (put, put) *v* /pʊt/ ★★★
quiz (-zes) *n C* /kwɪz/
shaved *adj* /ʃeɪvd/
short *adj* /ʃɔːt/ ★★★
smile *n C* /smaɪl/ ★★★
spiky *adj* /ˈspaɪki/

straight *adj* /streɪt/ ★★
sunglasses *npl* /ˈsʌnglɑːsɪz/
sweet *adj* /swiːt/ ★★
take (sth off) (took, taken) *v* /teɪk/ ★★★
tattoo *n C* /tæˈtuː/
try (sth on) (tried, tried) *v* /traɪ/ ★★★
wait (for sb/sth) *v* /weɪt/ ★★★
wave *v* /weɪv/ ★★
wavy *adj* /ˈweɪvi/
wear (wore, wore) *v* /weə/ ★★★

Unit 12

application form *n C* /æplɪˈkeɪʃ(ə)n fɔːm/
appointment *n C* /əˈpɔɪntmənt/ ★★★
believe (in sb/sth) *v* /bɪˈliːv/ ★★★
book *v* /bʊk/ ★
cope (with sb/sth) *v* /kəʊp/ ★★
definitely *adv* /ˈdefɪnətli/ ★★
diamond *adj* /ˈdaɪəmənd/
fairy tale *n C* /ˈfeəri teɪl/
future *adj* /ˈfjuːtʃə/ ★★★
future *n C* /ˈfjuːtʃə/ ★★★
hobby (-ies) *n C* /ˈhɒbi/
honeymoon *n C* /ˈhʌnɪmuːn/
hope *v* /həʊp/ ★★★
list *n C* /lɪst/ ★★★
photo album *n C* /ˈfəʊtəʊ ælbəm/
plan *n C* /plæn/ ★★★
positive *adj* /ˈpɒzɪtɪv/ ★★★
programme *n C* /ˈprəʊgræm/ ★★★

TV programmes

chat show *n C* /ˈtʃæt ʃəʊ/
documentary (-ies) *n C* /dɒkjʊˈmentəri/
game show *n C* /ˈgeɪm ʃəʊ/
news *n U* /njuːz/ ★★★
reality TV *n U* /riˈæləti tiː ˈviː/
soap opera *n C* /ˈsəʊp ɒp(ə)rə/
sports programme *n C* /ˈspɔːts prəʊgræm/
weather *n U* /ˈweðə/ ★★★

---

rose *n C* /rəʊz/ ★
stream *n C* /striːm/ ★
successful *adj* /səkˈsesfʊl/ ★★★
traditional *adj* /trəˈdɪʃ(ə)nəl/ ★★★

Unit 13

address book *n C* /əˈdres bʊk/
afford *v* /əˈfɔːd/ ★★★
bad *adj* /bæd/ ★★★
big *adj* /bɪg/ ★★★
bikini *n C* /bɪˈkiːniː/
bill *n C* /bɪl/ ★★★
busy *adj* /ˈbɪzi/ ★★★
cash *n U* /kæʃ/ ★★★
cheque *n C* /tʃek/ ★
debt *n C* /det/ ★★★
far *adj* /fɑː/ ★★★
fast *adj* /fɑːst/ ★★★
generous *adj* /ˈdʒen(ə)rəs/ ★

glove *n C* /glʌv/

handbag *n C* /'hæn(d)bæg/

hot *adj* /hɒt/ ★★★

hundred *num* /'hʌndrəd/ ★★

key *n C* /kiː/ ★★★

laptop computer *n C* /læptɒp kəm'pjuːtə/

lost property *n U* /lɒst 'prɒpəti/

lucky *adj* /'lʌki/ ★★

million *num* /'mɪljən/ ★

neighbour *n C* /'neɪbə/ ★★

object *n C* /'ɒbdʒɪkt/ ★★★

pay (sth/sb off) *v* /peɪ/ ★★★

poor *adj* /pɔː/ ★★★

popular *adj* /'pɒpjələ/ ★★★

quiet *adj* /'kwaɪət/ ★★★

relaxed *adj* /rɪ'lækst/ ★

save *v* /seɪv/ ★★★

save money /seɪv 'mʌni/

set (sth up) (set, set) *v* /set/ ★★★

size *n C* /saɪz/ ★★★

slow *adj* /sləʊ/ ★★★

snake *n C* /sneɪk/

swear (swore, sworn) *v* /sweə/ ★

tall *adj* /tɔːl/ ★★★

thousand *num* /'θaʊz(ə)nd/ ★★

TV remote *n C* /tiː viː rɪ'məʊt/

ugly *adj* /'ʌgli/ ★

violent *adj* /'vaɪələnt/ ★★★

website *n C* /'websaɪt/

wedding ring *n C* /'wedɪŋ rɪŋ/

young *adj* /jʌŋ/ ★★★

Unit 14

ancestry *n C* /'ænsəstri/

bend (bent, bent) *v* /bend/ ★★

body (-ies) *n C* /'bɒdi/ ★★★

Parts of the body

arm *n C* /ɑːm/ ★★★

back *n C* /bæk/ ★★★

chest *n C* /tʃest/ ★★★

chin *n C* /tʃɪn/ ★★

ear *n C* /ɪə/ ★★★

finger *n C* /'fɪŋgə/ ★★★

foot (feet) *n C* /fʊt/ ★★★

hand *n C* /hænd/ ★★★

heart *n C* /hɑːt/ ★★★

hip *n C* /hɪp/

knee *n C* /niː/ ★★★

leg *n C* /leg/ ★★★

lip *n C* /lɪp/ ★★★

neck *n C* /nek/ ★★★

nose *n C* /nəʊz/ ★★★

shoulder *n C* /'ʃəʊldə/ ★★★

stomach *n C* /'stʌmək/ ★★

thumb *n C* /θʌm/ ★

toe *n C* /təʊ/ ★

tooth (teeth) *n C* /tuːθ/ ★★★

waist *n C* /weɪst/

---

charming *adj* /'tʃɑːmɪŋ/

clap (clapped, clapped) *v* /klæp/

click *v* /klɪk/

cold *n C* /kəʊld/ ★★

cross *v* /krɒs/ ★★★

crowded *adj* /'kraʊdɪd/ ★

dominant *adj* /'dɒmɪnənt/

energy *n U* /'enədʒi/ ★★★

exciting *adj* /ɪk'saɪtɪŋ/ ★★

flamenco *n U* /flə'meŋkəʊ/

fold *v* /fəʊld/ ★★★

go dancing /gəʊ 'dɑːnsɪŋ/

gypsy (-es) *n C* /'dʒɪpsi/

hairdresser *n C* /'heədresə/

headache *n C* /'hedeɪk/ ★

impulsive *adj* /ɪm'pʌlsɪv/

loyal *adj* /'lɔɪəl/

nod (nodded, nodded) *v* /nɒd/ ★

once *adv* /wʌns/ ★★★

perform *v* /pə'fɔːm/ ★★★

performance *n C* /pə'fɔːməns/ ★★★

questionnaire *n C* /kwestʃə'neə/

score *n C* /skɔː/ ★★

selfish *adj* /'selfɪʃ/

shrug (shrugged, shrugged) *v* /ʃrʌg/

soul *n C* /səʊl/ ★

stamp *v* /stæmp/ ★

stomach ache *n C* /'stʌmək eɪk/

touch *v* /tʌtʃ/ ★★★

twice *adv* /twaɪs/ ★★★

unsociable *adj* /ʌn'səʊʃəb(ə)l/

Unit 15

changing room *n C* /'tʃeɪndʒɪŋ ruːm/

countryside *n C* /'kʌntrisaɪd/ ★★

go sightseeing /gəʊ 'saɪtsiːɪŋ/

have a day off /hæv ə deɪ 'ɒf/

noisy *adj* /'nɔɪsi/ ★

runner *n C* /'rʌnə/

safe *adj* /seɪf/ ★★★

suit *v* /suːt/ ★★★

Unit 16

band *n C* /bænd/ ★★★

classmate *n C* /'klɑːsmeɪt/

delete *v* /dɪ'liːt/

desktop *n C* /'desktɒp/

download *v* /daʊn'ləʊd/

drums *npl* /drʌmz/

employ *v* /ɪm'plɔɪ/ ★★

file *n C* /faɪl/

find (out) (found, found) *v* /faɪnd/ ★★★

garage *n C* /'gærɑːʒ, 'gærɪdʒ/ ★

get in touch (with sb/sth) *v* /get ɪn 'tʌtʃ/

give (sth up) (gave, given) *v* /gɪv/ ★★★

go online *v* /gəʊ ɒn'laɪn/

guitarist *n C* /gɪ'tɑːrɪst/

humour *n U* /'hjuːmə/

icon *n C* /'aɪkɒn/

internet *n C* /'ɪntənet/ ★★★

---

log on *v* /lɒg 'ɒn/

look (after sb/sth) *v* /lʊk/ ★★★

mouse (mouses/mice) *n C* /maʊs/

order *v* /'ɔːdə/ ★★★

personal organiser *n C* /pɜːsən(ə)l 'ɔːgənaɪzə/

pregnant *adj* /'pregnənt/ ★

primary school *n C* /'praɪməri skuːl/

publicity *n U* /pʌb'lɪs(ə)ti/ ★

record *v* /rɪ'kɔːd/ ★★★

reunion *n C* /riː'juːniən/

reunite *v* /riːjuː'naɪt/

screen *n C* /skriːn/ ★★

search (for sb/th) *v* /sɜːtʃ/ ★★

sell (sold, sold) *v* /sel/ ★★★

send (sent, sent) *v* /send/ ★★★

send an email /send ən 'iːmeɪl/

sense *n C* /sens/ ★★★

sense of humour *n C* /sens əv 'hjuːmə/

surf *v* /sɜːf/

surf the net /sɜːf ðə 'net/

take (sth on) (took, taken) *v* /teɪk/ ★★★

ticket *n C* /'tɪkɪt/ ★★★

toolbar *n C* /'tuːlbɑː/

word of mouth *n U* /wɜːd əv 'maʊθ/

Unit 17

coast *n* /kəʊst/ ★★

drive *n* /draɪv/ ★★

drive (drove, driven) *v* /draɪv/ ★★★

drive (sb) **mad** /draɪv sʌmbədi 'mæd/

get stuck /get 'stʌk/

go (went, been/gone) *v* /gəʊ/ ★★★

---

go + prepositions of movement

go across /gəʊ ə'krɒs/

go along /gəʊ ə'lɒŋ/

go down /gəʊ 'daʊn/

go into /gəʊ 'ɪntə/

go out of /gəʊ 'aʊt əv/

go over /gəʊ 'əʊvə/

go past /gəʊ 'pɑːst/

go straight on /gəʊ streɪt 'ɒn/

go through /gəʊ 'θruː/

go up /gəʊ 'ʌp/

---

have an accident /hæv ən 'æksɪdənt/

journey *n C* /'dʒɜːni/ ★★★

lighthouse *n C* /'laɪthaʊs/

motorway *n C* /'məʊtəweɪ/

Ordinal numbers

first *num* /fɜːst/ ★★★

second *num* /'sek(ə)nd/ ★★★

third *num* /θɜːd/ ★★★

fourth *num* /fɔːθ/

fifth *num* /fɪfθ/

sixth *num* /sɪksθ/

seventh *num* /'sev(ə)nθ/

eighth *num* /eɪtθ/

ninth *num* /naɪnθ/

tenth *num* /tenθ/

Based on data from the *Macmillan Essential Dictionary*

overtake (overtook, overtaken) *v* /ˌəʊvəˈteɪk/
pavement *n C* /ˈpeɪvmənt/ ★
pedestrian *n C* /pəˈdestriən/
plane *n C* /pleɪn/ ★★★
road works *npl* /ˈrəʊd wɜːks/
rush hour *n C* /ˈrʌʃ aʊə/
scenery *n U* /ˈsiːnəri/
set (off) (set, set) *v* /set/ ★★★
stand (stood, stood) *v* /stænd/ ★★★
– **I can't stand it when …**
/aɪ kɑːnt ˈstænd ɪt wen …/
traffic lights *npl* /ˈtræfɪk laɪts/
travel abroad *v* /ˈtræv(ə)l əˈbrɔːd/
turn left/right *v* /tɜːn ˈleft, raɪt/

Unit 18

angrily *adv* /ˈæŋgrɪli/
attractive *adj* /əˈtræktɪv/
attractively *adv* /əˈtræktɪvli/
badly *adv* /ˈbædli/ ★★
beautifully *adv* /ˈbjuːtɪf(ə)li/
careful *adj* /ˈkeəf(ə)l/ ★★★
carefully *adv* /ˈkeəf(ə)li/
castle *n C* /ˈkɑːs(ə)l/ ★★
catch (caught, caught) *v* /kætʃ/ ★★
differently *adv* /ˈdɪfrəntli/
dinner party (-ies) *n C* /ˈdɪnə pɑːti/
evil *adj* /ˈiːv(ə)l/
finally *adv* /ˈfaɪnəli/ ★★★
frog *n C* /frɒg/
have an affair /hæv ən əˈfeə/
justice *n U* /ˈdʒʌstɪs/ ★★
kiss (-es) *n C* /kɪs/ ★
loudly *adv* /ˈlaʊdli/
mystery play *n C* /ˈmɪstəri pleɪ/
next *adv* /nekst/ ★★★
once upon a time /ˈwʌns əpɒn ə ˈtaɪm/
paint *n U* /peɪnt/ ★
plastic *adj* /ˈplæstɪk/ ★★★
pond *n C* /pɒnd/
pot *n C* /pɒt/ ★★
prince *n C* /prɪns/
princess (-es) *n C* /prɪnˈses/
quick *adj* /kwɪk/ ★★★
quickly *adv* /ˈkwɪkli/ ★★★
quietly *adv* /ˈkwaɪətli/ ★★★
revenge *n U* /rɪˈvendʒ/
row *n C* /raʊ/ ★★★
salt *n U* /sɒlt/ ★
scissors *npl* /ˈsɪzəz/
shoplifter *n C* /ˈʃɒplɪftə/
stage *n C* /steɪdʒ/ ★★★
steal (stole, stolen) *v* /stiːl/ ★★
then *adv* /ðen/ ★★★
tidily *adv* /ˈtaɪdɪli/
tip *n C* /tɪp/ ★
unhappily *adv* /ʌnˈhæpɪli/
unhappy *adj* /ʌnˈhæpi/ ★★
usher *n C* /ˈʌʃə/
watch (-es) *n C* /wɒtʃ/ ★★

well *adv* /wel/ ★★★
whisper *v* /ˈwɪspə/ ★
wine *n U* /waɪn/ ★★★
witch (-es) *n C* /wɪtʃ/

Unit 19

Celsius *n U* /ˈselsiəs/
cliff *n C* /klɪf/
construct *v* /kənˈstrʌkt/ ★★
desert *n C* /ˈdezət/ ★★
design *v* /dɪˈzaɪn/ ★★★
extremely *adv* /ɪkˈstriːmli/ ★★★
field *n C* /fiːld/ ★★★
Geography *n U* /dʒɒgrəfi/
glacier *n C* /ˈglæsɪə, ˈgleɪsɪə/
ice *n U* /aɪs/ ★★
invite *v* /ɪnˈvaɪt/ ★★★
melt *v* /melt/ ★
month *n C* /mʌnθ/ ★★★
planet *n C* /ˈplænɪt/ ★
poem *n C* /ˈpəʊɪm/ ★
rainbow *n C* /ˈreɪnbəʊ/
reindeer *n C* /ˈreɪndɪə/
season *n C* /ˈsiːz(ə)n/ ★★★

Seasons

spring *n C* /sprɪŋ/ ★★
summer *n C* /ˈsʌmə/ ★★★
autumn *n C* /ˈɔːtəm/ ★★★
winter *n C* /ˈwɪntə/ ★★★

---

shore *n C* /ʃɔː/
situate *v* /ˈsɪtʃueɪt/
sleeping bag *n C* /ˈsliːpɪŋ bæg/
space *n U* /speɪs/ ★★★
sun *n U* /sʌn/ ★★★
temperature *n U* /ˈtemprɪtʃə/ ★★★
visitor *n C* /ˈvɪzɪtə/ ★★★
volcano (-es) *n C* /vɒlˈkeɪnəʊ/

Weather

cloud *n C* /klaʊd/ ★★★
cloudy *adj* /ˈklaʊdi/
cool *adj* /kuːl/ ★★★
dull *adj* /dʌl/ ★
fine *adj* /faɪn/ ★★★
fog *n U* /fɒg/
foggy *adj* /ˈfɒgi/
freezing *adj* /ˈfriːzɪŋ/
rain *n U* /reɪn/ ★★★
rain *v* /reɪn/ ★
rainy *adj* /ˈreɪni/
snow *n U* /snəʊ/ ★★
storm *n C* /stɔːm/ ★★
stormy *adj* /ˈstɔːmi/
wind *n U* /wɪnd/ ★★★
windy *adj* /ˈwɪndi/

---

weather forecast *n C* /ˈweðə fɔːkɑːst/

Unit 20

by bike / car / bus / train *adv*
/baɪ baɪk, kɑː, bʌs, treɪn/
continue *v* /kənˈtɪnjuː/ ★★★
film *v* /fɪlm/
film director *n C* /ˈfɪlm daɪrektə, dərektə/
lend (lent, lent) *v* /lend/ ★★★
monument *n C* /ˈmɒnjʊmənt/
Native American *n C* /neɪtɪv əˈmerɪk(ə)n/
on foot *adv* /ɒn ˈfʊt/
parking ticket *n C* /ˈpɑːkɪŋ tɪkɪt/
plan (planned, planned) *v* /plæn/ ★★★
scene *n C* /siːn/ ★★★
shake (shook, shaken) *v* /ʃeɪk/ ★★★
supermarket *n C* /ˈsuːpəmɑːkɪt/ ★
take part (in sth) *v* /teɪk ˈpɑːt/
woods *npl* /wʊdz/

Verb structures

Present simple
See Units 2 and 3.

Affirmative	Negative	Question	Short answer *Yes*	Short answer *No*
I/You/We/They **talk**.	I/You/We/They **don't** (**do not**) **talk**.	**Do** I/you/we/they **talk**?	Yes, I/you/we/they **do**.	No, I/you/we/they **don't**.
He/She/It **talks**.	He/She/It **doesn't** (**does not**) **talk**.	**Does** he/she/it **talk**?	Yes, he/she/it **does**.	No, he/she/it **doesn't**.

Present continuous
See Unit 11.

Affirmative	Negative	Question	Short answer *Yes*	Short answer *No*
I**'m** (**am**) **talking**.	I**'m not** (**am not**) **talking**.	**Am** I **talking**?	Yes, I **am**.	No, I**'m not**.
You/We/They**'re** (**are**) **talking**.	You/We/They**'re not** (**are not**) **talking**.	**Are** you/we/they **talking**?	Yes, you/we/they **are**.	No, you/we/they **aren't**.
He/She/It**'s** (**is**) **talking**.	He/She/It **isn't** (**is not**) **talking**.	**Is** he/she/it **talking**?	Yes, he/she/it **is**.	No, he/she/it **isn't**.

Note: When a verb ends with a single vowel letter followed by a single consonant letter, you usually double the final consonant letter before -*ing*: *chat* – *chatting*; *jog* – *jogging*; *refer* – *referring*; *stop* – *stopping*.

Present perfect simple
See Unit 16.

Affirmative	Negative	Question	Short answer *Yes*	Short answer *No*
I/You/We/They**'ve** (**have**) **talked**.	I/You/We/They **haven't** (**have not**) **talked**.	**Have** I/you/we/they **talked**?	Yes, I/you/we/they **have**.	No, I/you/we/they **haven't**.
He/She/It**'s** (**has**) **talked**.	He/She/It **hasn't** (**has not**) **talked**.	**Has** he/she/it **talked**?	Yes, he/she/it **has**.	No, he/she/it **hasn't**.

Note: See list of irregular verbs on page 117.

Past simple
See Units 8 and 9.

Affirmative	Negative	Question	Short answer *Yes*	Short answer *No*
I/You/He/She/It/We/They **talked**.	I/You/He/She/It/We/They **didn't** (**did not**) **talk**.	**Did** I/you/he/she/it/we/they **talk**?	Yes, I/you/he/she/it/we/they **did**.	No, I/you/he/she/it/we/they **didn't**.

Note: See list of irregular verbs on page 117.
Note: When a verb ends with a single vowel letter followed by a single consonant letter, you usually double the final consonant letter before -*ed*: *chat* – *chatted*; *jog* – *jogged*; *refer* – *referred*; *stop* – *stopped*.

Past continuous
See Unit 18.

Affirmative	Negative	Question	Short answer *Yes*	Short answer *No*
I/He/She/It **was talking**.	I/He/She/It **wasn't** (**was not**) **talking**.	**Was** I/he/she/it **talking**?	Yes, I/he/she/it **was**.	No, I/he/she/it **wasn't**.
You/We/They **were talking**.	You/We/They **weren't** (**were not**) **talking**.	**Were** you/we/they **talking**?	Yes, you/we/they **were**.	No, you/we/they **weren't**.

Future: *(be) going to*
See Unit 12.

Affirmative	Negative	Question	Short answer *Yes*	Short answer *No*
I'm (am) going to talk.	I'm not (am not) going to talk.	**Am** I **going to talk?**	Yes, I **am.**	No, I'm **not.**
You/We/They're (are) going to talk.	You/We/They're **not** (are not) going to talk.	**Are** you/we/they **going to talk?**	Yes, you/we/they **are.**	No, you/we/they **aren't.**
He/She/It's (is) going to talk.	He/She/It **isn't** (is not) going to talk.	**Is** he/she/it **going to talk?**	Yes, he/she/it **is.**	No, he/she/it **isn't.**

Modals

Affirmative	Negative	Question	Short answer *Yes*	Short answer *No*
can: see Unit 7. I/You/He, *etc.* **can talk.**	I/You/He, *etc.* **can't** (**cannot**) **talk.**	**Can** I/you/he, *etc.* **talk?**	Yes, I/you/he, *etc.* **can.**	No, I/you/he, *etc.* **can't.**
might: see Unit 19. I/You/He, *etc.* **might talk.**	I/You/He, *etc.* **mightn't** (**might not**) **talk.**	**Might** I/you/he, *etc.* **talk?**	Yes, I/you/he, *etc.* **might.**	No, I/you/he, *etc.* **might not.**
should: see Unit 14. I/You/He, *etc.* **should talk.**	I/You/He, *etc.* **shouldn't** (**should not**) **talk.**	**Should** I/you/he, *etc.* **talk?**	Yes, I/you/he, *etc.* **should.**	No, I/you/he, *etc.* **shouldn't.**
will: see Unit 19. I/You/He, *etc.* **'ll** (**will**) **talk.**	I/You/He, *etc.* **won't** (**will not**) **talk.**	**Will** I/you/he, *etc.* **talk?**	Yes, I/you/he, *etc.* **will.**	No, I/you/he, *etc.* **won't.**
would: see Unit 6. I/You/He, *etc.* **'d** (**would**) **talk.**	I/You/He, *etc.* **wouldn't** (**would not**) **talk.**	**Would** I/you/he, *etc.* **talk?**	Yes, I/you/he, *etc.* **would.**	No, I/you/he, *etc.* **wouldn't.**

Active & passive forms
See Unit 19.

	Active form	Passive form
Present	Somebody **produces** cars.	Cars **are produced.**
Past	Somebody **produced** cars.	Cars **were produced.**

Adjectives

Comparatives
See Unit 13.

+ *-er* / *-r*	double letter + *-er*	– *y* + *-ier*	irregular	*more* + adjective
rich → rich**er** nice → nic**er**	big → big**ger**	lucky → luck**ier**	good → **better** bad → **worse** far → **further**	generous → **more** generous

Superlatives
See Unit 13.

+ *-est* / *-st*	double letter + *-est*	– *y* + *-iest*	irregular	*more* + adjective
rich → the rich**est** nice → the nic**est**	big → the big**gest**	lucky → the luck**iest**	good → the **best** bad → the **worst** far → the **furthest**	generous → the **most** generous

Grammar glossary

```
                          modal
                          auxiliary              article
main                      verb                                  main
verb    adjective         adverb         pronoun                verb
```

Learn these useful words and you can understand more about the language you are studying.

```
        noun   pronoun   main verb   preposition   noun   auxiliary
                                                          verb
```

Collocation refers to words that frequently occur together.
> For example: *common sense get on well Merry Christmas*

Expressions are groups of words that belong together where the words and word order never or rarely change.
> For example: ***black and white   That reminds me**, I must buy some toothpaste.*
> ***How do you do?***

Objects usually come after the verb and show who or what is affected by the verb.
> For example: *She closed **the window**.   My neighbour hates **me**.   I've made **a cup of tea**.*

Particles are adverbs or prepositions that form part of a phrasal verb.
> For example: *sit **down**   switch **off**   look **after***

Phrasal verbs are verbs consisting of a main verb + particle(s). Phrasal verbs are sometimes referred to as 'multi-word verbs'.
> For example: ***find out**   I want **to set** a website **up**.*
> *I sometimes **look after** my neighbour's pet.*

Subjects usually come before the verb and refer to the main person or thing you are talking about.
> For example: ***Money** doesn't grow on trees.   **My tailor** is rich.*
> ***The biggest rock and roll group in the world** have started their world tour.*

Classroom language

The classroom

What's that in English?
What's this in English?
answer bag board book cassette/CD player chair definition desk dictionary door map pen picture piece of paper question sentence student teacher window word

Teacher language

Work with a partner / in groups of three.
Look at the board / photograph.
Listen to the conversation / song.
Write the answers / your name on a piece of paper.
Read the text / article.
Use your dictionary / a piece of paper.

Student language

How do you say … in English?
How do you spell it?
Can you repeat that?
I don't understand.
What does … mean?

Numbers

0	zero / nought	16	sixteen
1	one	17	seventeen
2	two	18	eighteen
3	three	19	nineteen
4	four	20	twenty
5	five	21	twenty-one
6	six	30	thirty
7	seven	40	forty
8	eight	50	fifty
9	nine	60	sixty
10	ten	70	seventy
11	eleven	80	eighty
12	twelve	90	ninety
13	thirteen	100	a hundred
14	fourteen	1,000	a thousand
15	fifteen	1,000,000	a million

Phonetic symbols

SINGLE VOWELS

/ɪ/	big fish	/bɪg fɪʃ/
/iː/	green beans	/griːn biːnz/
/ʊ/	should look	/ʃʊd lʊk/
/uː/	blue moon	/bluː muːn/
/e/	ten eggs	/ten egz/
/ə/	about mother	/əbaʊt mʌðə/
/ɜː/	learn words	/lɜːn wɜːdz/
/ɔː/	short talk	/ʃɔːt tɔːk/
/æ/	fat cat	/fæt kæt/
/ʌ/	must come	/mʌst kʌm/
/ɑː/	calm start	/kɑːm stɑːt/
/ɒ/	hot spot	/hɒt spɒt/

DIPHTHONGS

/ɪə/	ear	/ɪə/
/eɪ/	face	/feɪs/
/ʊə/	pure	/pjʊə/
/ɔɪ/	boy	/bɔɪ/
/əʊ/	nose	/nəʊz/
/eə/	hair	/heə/
/aɪ/	eye	/aɪ/
/aʊ/	mouth	/maʊθ/

CONSONANTS

/p/	pen	/pen/
/b/	bad	/bæd/
/t/	tea	/tiː/
/d/	dog	/dɒg/
/tʃ/	church	/tʃɜːtʃ/
/dʒ/	jazz	/dʒæz/
/k/	cost	/kɒst/
/g/	girl	/gɜːl/
/f/	far	/fɑː/
/v/	voice	/vɔɪs/
/θ/	thin	/θɪn/
/ð/	then	/ðen/
/s/	snake	/sneɪk/
/z/	noise	/nɔɪz/
/ʃ/	shop	/ʃɒp/
/ʒ/	measure	/meʒə/
/m/	make	/meɪk/
/n/	nine	/naɪn/
/ŋ/	sing	/sɪŋ/
/h/	house	/haʊs/
/l/	leg	/leg/
/r/	red	/red/
/w/	wet	/wet/
/j/	yes	/jes/

STRESS

In this book, word stress is shown by underlining the stressed syllable.
For example: water; result; disappointing

LETTERS OF THE ALPHABET

/eɪ/	/iː/	/e/	/aɪ/	/əʊ/	/uː/	/ɑː/
Aa	Bb	Ff	Ii	Oo	Qq	Rr
Hh	Cc	Ll	Yy		Uu	
Jj	Dd	Mm			Ww	
Kk	Ee	Nn				
	Gg	Ss				
	Pp	Xx				
	Tt	Zz				
	Vv					

Irregular verbs

Infinitive	Past simple	Past participle
be	was/were	been
beat	beat	beaten
become	became	become
begin	began	begun
bend	bent	bent
bet	bet	bet
bite	bit	bitten
blow	blew	blown
break	broke	broken
bring	brought	brought
build	built	built
burn	burnt/burned	burnt/burned
burst	burst	burst
buy	bought	bought
can	could	(been able)
catch	caught	caught
choose	chose	chosen
come	came	come
cost	cost	cost
cut	cut	cut
deal	dealt	dealt
do	did	done
draw	drew	drawn
dream	dreamt/dreamed	dreamt/dreamed
drink	drank	drunk
drive	drove	driven
eat	ate	eaten
fall	fell	fallen
feed	fed	fed
feel	felt	felt
fight	fought	fought
find	found	found
fly	flew	flown
forget	forgot	forgotten
forgive	forgave	forgiven
freeze	froze	frozen
get	got	got
give	gave	given
go	went	gone/been
grow	grew	grown
hang	hung/hanged	hung/hanged
have	had	had
hear	heard	heard
hide	hid	hidden
hit	hit	hit
hold	held	held
hurt	hurt	hurt
keep	kept	kept
kneel	knelt/kneeled	knelt/kneeled
know	knew	known
lay	laid	laid
lead	led	led
learn	learnt/learned	learnt/learned
leave	left	left
lend	lent	lent
let	let	let

Infinitive	Past simple	Past participle
lie	lay/lied	lied/lain
light	lit/lighted	lit/lighted
lose	lost	lost
make	made	made
mean	meant	meant
meet	met	met
must	had to	(had to)
pay	paid	paid
put	put	put
read	read /red/	read /red/
ride	rode	ridden
ring	rang	rung
rise	rose	risen
run	ran	run
say	said	said
see	saw	seen
sell	sold	sold
send	sent	sent
set	set	set
shake	shook	shaken
shine	shone	shone
shoot	shot	shot
show	showed	shown
shrink	shrank	shrunk
shut	shut	shut
sing	sang	sung
sink	sank	sunk
sit	sat	sat
sleep	slept	slept
slide	slid	slid
smell	smelt/smelled	smelt/smelled
speak	spoke	spoken
spell	spelt/spelled	spelt/spelled
spend	spent	spent
spill	spilt/spilled	spilt/spilled
split	split	split
spoil	spoilt/spoiled	spoilt/spoiled
spread	spread	spread
stand	stood	stood
steal	stole	stolen
stick	stuck	stuck
swear	swore	sworn
swell	swelled	swollen/swelled
swim	swam	swum
take	took	taken
teach	taught	taught
tear	tore	torn
tell	told	told
think	thought	thought
throw	threw	thrown
understand	understood	understood
wake	woke	woken
wear	wore	worn
win	won	won
write	wrote	written

Tapescripts

Unit 0

🔊 **01**

a) a picture
b) a window
c) the board
d) a word
e) a definition
f) a sentence
g) a question
h) an answer
i) a teacher
j) a map
k) the door
l) the cassette player
m) a student
n) a chair
o) a piece of paper
p) a dictionary
q) a pen
r) a desk
s) a book
t) a bag

🔊 **02**

Point to the board.
Point to the door.
Point to a chair.
Point to a book.
Point to a desk.
Point to a window.
Point to the cassette player.
Point to a student.
Point to a bag.
Point to the teacher.

🔊 **03**

a) Work with a partner.
b) Look at the board.
c) Listen to the conversation.
d) Write the answers on a piece of paper.
e) Read the text.
f) Use your dictionary.

🔊 **04**

(St A = Student A; T = Teacher;
St B = Student B)
St A: How do you say *compañero* in
English?
T: 'Partner'
St A: How do you spell it?
T: P-A-R-T-N-E-R
St A: Can you repeat that?
T: P-A-R-T-N-E-R
St A: Okay ... You're my partner.
St B: Uh ... I don't understand.
St A: You - are - my - partner.
St B: What does 'partner' mean?
St A: 'Compañero'!

Unit 1

🔊 **05**

(L = Lina; M = Mike)
L: Good afternoon. Can I help you?
M: Yes, I'd like to join the club, please.
L: Certainly. I just need to ask you a few
questions. What's your first name?
M: Mike.
L: And what's your surname?
M: Turnbull.
L: How do you spell that, please?
M: T-U-R-N-B-U-double L.
L: Okay. Now, your address, where do
you live?
M: 23 Trinity Road, London SW18.
L: Lovely. And what's your telephone
number?
M: 09732 176 double 7 3.
L: Sorry, can you repeat that?
M: Yes – 09732 176 double 7 3.
L: Okay. How old are you?
M: I'm 27.
L: 27. And what do you do?
M: I'm an engineer. I work for a mobile
phone company.
L: Oh, very nice. And are you married?
M: No, I'm not. I'm single.
L: Okay. Last question. What are you
interested in: gym, aerobics,
swimming, yoga, tennis, squash,
boxing or tai chi?
M: Um, gym, squash and tai chi. And
maybe tennis.
L: Lovely.

🔊 **06**

a) What's your first name?
b) What's your surname?
c) Where do you live?
d) What's your telephone number?
e) How old are you?
f) What do you do?
g) Are you married?
h) What are you interested in?

🔊 **07**

(K = Kate; L = Lina)
K: Ooh, he's nice!
L: Hm, he's okay.
K: What's his name?
L: Mike.
K: Ooh, I like the name Mike. What does
he do?
L: He's an engineer.
K: Ooh, really? How old is he?
L: Kate!
K: What?
L: He's 27.
K: Where does he live?
L: In Trinity Road.
K: Is he ...
L: What?
K: Is he married?
L: Yes.
K: Oh.

L: Actually, he isn't married. He's
single.
K: What's his telephone number?
L: Kate!

🔊 **08**

/ /: A H J K
/ :/: B C D E G P T V
/ /: F L M N S X Z
/ /: I Y
/ /: O
/ :/: Q U W
/ :/: R

🔊 **09**

1 E I A U O
2 I U A O E
3 A I O E U
4 A E I O U
5 I A O U E

🔊 **10**

1 UFO   5 VIP
2 CNN   6 IOC
3 BBC   7 UN
4 CIA   8 IBM

🔊 **11**

(L = Lina; S = Stewart; C = Claire;
G = Graeme; K = Kathryn)

a)
L: What's your name?
S: Stewart.
L: Is that S T U A R T?
S: No, it's S T E W A R T.
L: Okay, thanks.

b)
L: What's your name?
C: Claire.
L: Is that C L A R E?
C: No, it's C L A I R E.
L: Okay, thanks.

c)
L: What's your name?
G: Graeme.
L: Is that G R A H A M?
G: No, it's G R A E M E.
L: Okay, thanks.

d)
L: What's your name?
K: Kathryn.
L: Is that K A T H R Y N?
K: Yes, it is.
L: Oh ... great. Er ... Thanks.

🔊 **12**

(See page 7.)

13

Here are some useful numbers for travellers in the UK.

For flight information to and from Heathrow airport dial oh eight seven oh, oh double oh, oh one two three.

For UK train times dial oh eight four five, seven four eight, four nine five oh.

For National Express bus and coach information ring oh eight seven oh, five eight oh, eight oh eight oh.

Hertz Car Rental is oh two oh, double eight nine seven, two oh seven two.

And the British Tourist Authority can help you with other information. Dial oh two oh, double eight four six, nine oh double oh.

14

a)
'Are you Spanish?'
'Yes, I am.'
'No, I'm not.'

b)
'Do you live near here?'
'Yes, I do.'
'No, I don't.'

c)
'Have you got any brothers and sisters?'
'Yes, I have.'
'No, I haven't.'

d)
'Are you married?'
'Yes, I am.'
'No, I'm not.'

e)
'Do you like Italian food?'
'Yes, I do.'
'No, I don't.'

f)
'Have you got a motorbike?'
'Yes, I have.'
'No, I haven't.'

g)
'Do you like watching television?'
'Yes, I do.'
'No, I don't.'

15

She's Got You

I've got your picture
That you gave to me,
And it's signed with love
Just like it used to be.

The only thing different,
The only thing new:
I've got your picture,
She's got you.

I've got the records
That we used to share.
And they still sound the same
As when you were here.

The only thing different,
The only thing new:
I've got the records,
She's got you.

I've got your memory,
Or has it got me?
I really don't know.
But I know
It won't let me be.

I've got your class ring
That proved you cared.
And it still looks the same
As when you gave it, dear.

The only thing different,
The only thing new:
I've got these little things,
She's got you.

Unit 2

16

a) My mother is a nurse. She works in a hospital.
b) My father is an engineer. He works for a big construction company.
c) My cousin is a DJ. He works in a night club.
d) My friend is a secretary. She works in an office.
e) My uncle is a mechanic. He works for his father.

17

(B = Beth; A = Angie)
B: This is me with my brother.
A: Oh, he's nice. Is he married?
B: No, he isn't. He's single.
A: Has he got a girlfriend?
B: No, he hasn't.
A: Oh. What does he do?
B: He's a doctor.
A: Oh. Does he live near here?
B: No, he doesn't. He lives in Australia, actually.
A: Oh. Is this your father?
B: No, that's my boyfriend.
A: Oh, sorry.

18

a)
'Are you a student at university?'
'Yes, I am.'
'No, I'm not.'

b)
'Have you got a part-time job?'
'Yes, I have.'
'No, I haven't.'

c)
'Do you work in an office?'
'Yes, I do.'
'No, I don't.'

d)
'Is your grandfather retired?'
'Yes, he is.'
'No, he isn't.'

e)
'Has your father got an interesting job?'
'Yes, he has.'
'No, he hasn't.'

f)
'Does your mother speak English?'
'Yes, she does.'
'No, she doesn't.'

g)
'Do you play the piano?'
'Yes, I do.'
'No, I don't.'

h)
'Does your grandmother live near you?'
'Yes, she does.'
'No, she doesn't.'

19

(B = Beth; A = Angie)
B: This is Amy. She's my sister.
A: Oh – older sister or younger sister?
B: Older!
A: Oh! Where does she live?
B: In the city centre. She lives with her husband and her baby boy.
A: Ah. What's her baby's name?
B: Brad. He's lovely.
A: Oh. So, is Amy a housewife?
B: No, she's a teacher. She works in a school in the city centre. She's a French teacher.
A: Oh.
B: And this is Robert. He's my favourite cousin.
A: Wow, he's nice.
B: I know. He lives in San Francisco.
A: Oh no, why?
B: He's an actor. Well, he's an actor and a waiter. He works in an Italian restaurant. But he's a very good actor.
A: Is he married?
B: No, no, he isn't married but he's got lovely friends.
A: How often do you see him?
B: I see him every year.

20

Think about one of your relatives.
Is it a man or a woman?
What's his or her name?
What relation is he or she to you?
Where does he or she live?
What does he or she do?
Is he or she married
Has he or she got children?
What do you do and what do you talk about when you see him or her?

21

Argentina, Argentinian, Spanish
Brazil, Brazilian, Portuguese
France, French, French
Germany, German, German
Italy, Italian, Italian
Japan, Japanese, Japanese
Poland, Polish, Polish
Spain, Spanish, Spanish
the United Kingdom, British, English
the United States of America, American, English

Unit 3

22

We asked people in the street: 'What do you do when you want to relax?' Here are some of the answers.
1 'I have a cup of tea and watch television. I watch films and sport.'
2 'I listen to the radio and do the washing up.'
3 'I have a nice long bath.'
4 'I go to the park with my son.'
5 'I listen to music and do yoga.'
6 'I go for a walk and listen to the birds singing.'
7 'I go swimming and then I have lunch with friends.'
8 'I do the ironing or I watch a video.'

23

(See page 15.)

24

Ending with /s/: acts, laughs, takes
Ending with /z/: needs, pays, wins
Ending with /ɪz/: finishes, relaxes, teaches

25

(W = Woman; M = Man)

W: I cry, he laughs.
M: I give, she takes.
W: I think, he acts.
M&W: We're different.

M: I want, she needs.
W: I spend, he pays.
M: I lose, she wins.
M&W: We're different.

M: I learn, she teaches.
W: I work, he relaxes.
M: I start, she finishes.
M&W: We're married!

26

Jack loves water, really likes being outside, really likes sport, hates towns and cities and doesn't like loud music. He loves playing football, swimming, jogging and going to the gym. But he doesn't like shopping, clubbing, eating out in restaurants or going to rock concerts. … Oh, and he really likes Layla.

Layla loves spending money, doesn't like being outside, hates doing housework but doesn't mind cooking, likes dancing but hates sport. She loves shopping, clubbing, eating out in restaurants and going to rock concerts. But she doesn't like playing football, swimming, jogging or going to the gym. … And Jack? She really likes him.

Unit 4

27

a) In a kitchen: blinds, cooker, cupboard, dishwasher, fridge, radiator, sink, washing machine
b) In a bedroom: bed, curtains, carpet or rug, cushions, lamp, mirror, picture, radiator, shelf / shelves, wardrobe
c) In a bathroom: bath, mirror, radiator, shower, washbasin

28

a)
'Is there a fireplace in your living room?'
'Yes, there is.'
'No, there isn't.'

b)
'Are there any posters on your bedroom walls?'
'Yes, there are.'
'No, there aren't.'

c)
'Are there any plants in your kitchen?'
'Yes, there are.'
'No, there aren't.'

d)
'Is there a carpet on your bathroom floor?'
'Yes, there is.'
'No, there isn't.'

e)
'Is there a park near your home?'
'Yes, there is.'
'No, there isn't.'

f)
'Are there any good shops near your home?'
'Yes, there are.'
'No, there aren't.'

29

Think about your home.
You are walking to your home. Are you in the city or the country?
You are in front of your home. Is it a house or a flat? Is it old or modern?
What colour is the front door? Is there a number on it? What is the number?
You open the door and go inside. What can you see?
You go into the kitchen. Is it light or dark? What is there in the kitchen?
You go into the living room. Is it big or small? What furniture is there?
Now you go into your bedroom. Is it tidy? What furniture is there?
You open the window and look out. What can you see from your window?

Unit 5

30

(R = Receptionist; C = Client)
R: Good afternoon. Palm Beach Hotel.
C: Hello. I'd like to book a room, with a beautiful view.
R: All our rooms have beautiful views, madam. The hotel is on the beach. There are palm trees and wonderful beaches and little fishing boats …
C: Oh, oh, that's nice, but …
R: There's the sun and the sea …
C: Oh good, good. But are there any shops near the hotel?
R: There aren't any clouds in the clear blue sky …
C: Um, are there any restaurants or clubs?
R: Restaurants or clubs? Er … no, madam, there aren't. At the Palm Beach Hotel there are palm trees and wonderful beaches and little fishing …
C: Okay, thank you. Goodbye.

31

A: chocolate, different, evening, listening, Wednesday
B: interesting, miserable, restaurant, secretary, vegetable
C: decision, delicious, mechanic, reception, relation

32

a)   There's a clock next to the radiator.
b)   There's a mirror on the wall above the bookcase.
c)   There are some photos on the bookcase.
d)   There's a lamp in the corner.
e)   There are some flowers under the desk.
f)   There's a rug on the floor.

33

a)   What's your name?
b)   Have you got any children?
c)   Do you like watching football?
d)   Where do you live?
e)   Are you married?
f)   Why do you want to work here?

34

(See page 25.)

Unit 6

35

(See page 26.)

36

(A = Alan; K = Kathryn)
A: I want to lose weight but I love my food. How do you stay so slim?
K: I follow the food combining rules.
A: Food combining? What's that?
K: Well, for example, I never eat protein and carbohydrates together.
A: What? Do you mean you never eat steak and chips?
K: No, because steak is protein and chips are carbohydrates.
A: Oh. What about fish and rice. That's healthy.
K: No, fish is protein and rice is carbohydrate. Fish and vegetables is okay.
A: Well, how about my favourite meal – spaghetti bolognese with fruit salad for dessert.
K: No, sorry. There's meat in bolognese and spaghetti is carbohydrate. And you can't eat fruit as a dessert.

A: Oh dear. I don't like this. My favourite diet is the seafood diet.
K: Oh, what's that?
A: When you see food, you eat it.
K&A: Ha ha ha.

▭ 37

a)
'Are there any mushrooms in picture C?'
'Yes, there are.'
'No, there aren't.'

b)
'Is there any cheese in picture A?'
'Yes, there is.'
'No, there isn't.'

c)
'Is there a cauliflower in picture C?'
'Yes, there is.'
'No, there isn't.'

d)
'Is there any pasta in picture B?'
'Yes, there is.'
'No, there isn't.'

e)
'Are there any bananas in picture A?'
'Yes, there are.'
'No, there aren't.'

f)
'Is there any bread in picture D?'
'Yes, there is.'
'No, there isn't.'

▭ 38

Okay, let's see now. What do we need for P Diddy's dressing room? Ummm … Four cartons of fruit juice, twelve bottles of mineral water … Okay. Two bottles of Cristal champagne and two bottles of white wine … Right. Twenty bars of soap and ninety-six hand towels … Yep, all there …

Now how about Jennifer Lopez? Er … A white room with white furniture … Yeah, that's okay. Some white candles, a vase of white flowers and a bottle of Evian water … No problem. Some vanilla ice-cream and a packet of chocolate biscuits … Yep, fine.

And last but not least, Mariah Carey … Pink toilet paper … Okay. Two bottles of Cristal champagne, a bowl of fresh fruit and twelve bottles of Poland spring water … *Poland* spring water?! All right … Some little trees with lights on? And what's this … kittens and puppies to play with!!! … Whatever next!

▭ 39

a)
'How much milk have you got?'
'I've got a lot.'
'I haven't got much.'
'I haven't got any.'

b)
'How many tomatoes have you got?'
'I've got a lot.'
'I haven't got many.'
'I haven't got any.'

c)
'How much cheese have you got?'
'I've got a lot.'
'I haven't got much.'
'I haven't got any.'

d)
'How many peppers have you got?'
'I've got a lot.'
'I haven't got many.'
'I haven't got any.'

▭ 40

(SA = Shop assistant; C = Customer)
SA: Next!
C: I'd like a chicken sandwich, please.
SA: Would you like brown or white bread, butter or margarine, mustard or mayonnaise, salt and pepper?
C: I'd like … a chicken sandwich.
SA: Yes, I know you'd like a chicken sandwich. But would you like brown bread or white bread, butter …
C: STOP, STOP. Can you speak more slowly, please?
SA: Would you like white or brown bread?
C: Er … brown bread, please.
SA: Would you like butter or margarine?
C: Butter.
SA: Would you like mustard or mayonnaise?
C: Mayonnaise.
SA: Would you like salt and pepper?
C: No, thank you.
SA: Would you like anything to drink?
C: Anything to drink? What is 'anything to drink'?
SA: Coke, orange juice, water …
C: Ah, drink, drink – coke, orange juice, water. Yes, yes, I understand. No.
SA: That's two dollars. … Next!

Unit 7

▭ 41

A: practical, serious, sociable
B: ambitious, creative, hard-working, romantic
C: adventurous
D: energetic, independent

▭ 42

Interview A
(I = Interviewer; C = Cherry Tree)
I: Cherry Tree, your new film is a big hit. How do you feel?
C: I feel terrible.
I: Sorry?
C: I feel terrible because I hate being famous. It's boring. I have to go to parties. I have to sign autographs.
I: But you're …
C: I have to wear make-up all day. I have to kiss Brad Pitt.
I: Oh dear. That's terrible. But you're rich now. You can buy anything you want.
C: Yes, but there are photographers everywhere. I can't walk down the street. I can't go shopping. I can't go clubbing and I can't have a private life.
I: Well, why did you make the film?
C: And I have to answer stupid questions!

Interview B
(I = Interviewer; M = Max Nova)
I: Max Nova, can you answer a few questions?
M: Sure, no problem.
I: Your film is a big success. How do you feel?
M: I feel fantastic. I love being rich, and I love being famous!
I: Now that you're rich and famous, is your life very different?
M: Oh yeah, very different. I don't have to worry about money any more. I can buy anything I want. I can buy a new car, I can buy a big house, I can travel first class… and I can meet some very interesting people.

▭ 43

Think about someone who has a good job.
What is his or her name?
What does he or she do?
Where does he or she work?
Who does he or she work for?
What time does he or she start and finish work?
How much does he or she earn?
How much does he or she travel?
Would you like this job?

Unit 8

▭ 44

(I = Interviewer; P = Pete; S = Shanaz; N = Nacho)

1 Pete
I: Excuse me. I'm from a new sports shop. Can I ask you some questions about water sports?
P: Sure.
I: Em, what's your name?
P: It's Pete.
I: Okay, Pete, do you ever go swimming?
P: Oh yes, I love swimming.
I: And when was the last time you went swimming?
P: Em, in August. I was on holiday.
I: And do you ever go sailing?
P: No – I'd like to, but I don't know anybody with a boat.
I: Okay, how about other water sports?
P: I sometimes go windsurfing.
I: When was the last time you went windsurfing?
P: Last summer with my friend. We were on holiday.
I: Great. Well, come along to our shop some time. Here's the address.
P: Yeah, thanks.

2 Shanaz
I: Excuse me. I'm from a new sports shop. Can I ask you some questions about water sports?
S: Oh, okay.
I: What's your name?
S: Shanaz.
I: Right, Shanaz, do you ever go swimming?
S: No. I can't swim.
I: Oh, I see. Um, do you ever go sailing?
S: Yeah, I go on my friend's boat.

I: Oh good, and when was the last time you went sailing?
S: About six weeks ago.
I: And do you do other water sports?
S: No, I told you, I can't swim.
I: Oh, right. Thank you.

3 Nacho
I: Excuse me. I'm from a new sports shop. Can I ask you some questions about water sports?
N: Water sports?
I: Yes, what's your name?
N: Nacho Fernandez Almira Olivera.
I: Okay, em, Nacho, do you ever go swimming?
N: Yes, yes, a lot.
I: Oh great. When was the last time you went swimming?
N: Yesterday.
I: Right, and do you ever go sailing?
N: Yes, but not often.
I: When was the last time you went sailing?
N: I can't remember. A long time ago.
I: Do you ever do other water sports?
N: Yes, I love scuba-diving.
I: Wow. When was the last time you went scuba-diving?
N: Last year. In Egypt.
I: Lovely. Well, our new shop is in the centre of town …

📼 45

A: **Same syllables**
work – worked; use – used;
stop – stopped; open – opened;
love – loved; discover – discovered;
ask – asked

B: **Extra syllable**
want – wanted; start – started;
point – pointed

📼 46

a) went, did, sent
b) had, sold, told
c) brought, swam, thought
d) met, let, got
e) read, heard, said
f) could, taught, caught
g) flew, knew, bought
h) saw, kept, slept

📼 47

And here are the words for tonight's bingo.
meant, meant stole, stole
drank, drank wore, wore hit, hit
woke, woke fought, fought gave, gave
won, won forgot, forgot grew, grew
chose, chose ran, ran paid, paid
cost, cost understood, understood
lent, lent cut, cut spent, spent
began, began threw, threw felt, felt
stood, stood became, became
learnt, learnt met, met built, built
made, made sang, sang rang, rang

📼 48

Shark attack!
When he was eight, British actor, Richard E Grant went on holiday to Mozambique with his parents and his younger brother. One day, they went fishing in a small motor boat on an enormous lagoon called San Martina. After a few hours, the motor stopped, and they couldn't start it again. They shouted, but nobody heard them. Suddenly, something moved in the water near the boat.

At first, they thought it was a dolphin. But then they realised it was a big, grey shark. It started knocking the boat. The boat rocked from side to side, and they nearly fell into the water. They were terrified. Grant's father tried to push the shark away, and his mother held him and his brother. They thought they were going to die.

Eventually, people in a fishing boat heard them and took them home. Everybody in the town heard about their story and talked about it. Grant's father became a local hero. Two or three weeks later, a local fisherman caught the shark and put it in the main square. Everybody came to see the monster and took pictures of it.

Many years later, when Grant saw the film *Jaws*, he relived the terrible experience.

📼 49

(F = Frank; L = Lottie)
F: I don't know where to go on holiday this year. Where did you go for your last summer holiday?
L: I went to the beach – to Tarifa in the South of Spain.
F: Oh, lovely. When did you go there?
L: Um, in July.
F: Nice. Who did you go with?
L: My sister and a friend.
F: Oh, yes. How did you get there?
L: We flew from London to Malaga, and then we drove from Malaga to Tarifa. There's a really good motorway.
F: Great. Where did you stay?
L: In the Hurricane Hotel. Do you know it?
F: No – what's it like?
L: Fantastic. The rooms are wonderful. And it's near the beach.
F: Mm, you are lucky. How long did you stay?
L: Just two weeks, unfortunately.
F: Oh, well. So what did you do all day?
L: We went to the beach, of course – you can do everything there. I tried kitesurfing – it's amazing.
F: Wow – I suppose you were tired in the evening.
L: Yes, but we went out a lot too – there are some really good tapas bars and clubs in Tarifa.
F: Mm, and did you meet anybody nice?
L: Well, yes, I did actually. He's a windsurfing instructor, and the first time we went out …

Unit 9

📼 50

(See page 38.)

📼 51

(I = Interviewer; N = Nelly B)
I: Welcome to this week's edition of *Heroes*. Today we have the popular television presenter, Nelly B, in the studio. Nelly, hello and welcome.
N: Thank you. It's lovely to be here.
I: Nelly, who is your hero and why?
N: My hero is Debra Veal because she spent 113 days alone at sea in a rowing boat.
I: Yes, that is pretty amazing, isn't it? Why did she do it?
N: Well, that's a good question. She started a trans-Atlantic race with her husband, Andrew, but he left after two weeks. He was frightened of the ocean.
I: How did she feel when Andrew left her?
N: I think she was relieved when he left. She just wanted him to be happy and healthy again.
I: What was the main danger of being alone on the boat?
N: It was difficult for her to sleep, because she was frightened of big ships. The tankers are enormous and they can't see a small boat.
I: Did she have any bad experiences?
N: She was frightened of sharks, and one night there was a very big one under the boat – but it wasn't interested in her – it was only interested in eating the fish under the boat.
I: Did she feel lonely?
N: Very lonely. Before the trip, she never spent time alone. She has an identical twin who was with her for the first twenty years of her life, and then she met Andrew.
I: What did she miss most?
N: Well, of course she missed people. But the other thing was fresh food. She missed vegetables and salad. And glasses of red wine.
I: Was Andrew there when she arrived in Barbados?
N: Oh yes, of course. Andrew was there to meet her with a bottle of champagne.
I: And she deserved it! Nelly, thank you so much. Debra Veal is an inspiration. Next week we'll be talking to …

📼 52

A: think – thought know – knew
feel – felt mean – meant
speak – spoke see – saw
B: fight – fought wake – woke
spend – spent grow – grew
wear – wore spell – spelt

📼 53

thought – fought knew – grew
felt – spelt meant – spent spoke – woke
saw – wore

54

a)
'Was the weather good yesterday?'
'Yes, it was.'
'No, it wasn't.'

b)
'Did you get up early?'
'Yes, I did.'
'No, I didn't.'

c)
'Did you have a bath?'
'Yes, I did.'
'No, I didn't.'

d)
'Did your mother make breakfast for you?'
'Yes, she did.'
'No, she didn't.'

e)
'Were you late for work or school?'
'Yes, I was.'
'No, I wasn't.'

f)
'Did your friends call or text you?'
'Yes, they did.'
'No, they didn't.'

g)
'Did you go out in the evening?'
'Yes, I did.'
'No, I didn't.'

Unit 10

55

(See page 42.)

56

a) How much money did you spend the last time you went out?
b) How many emails did you receive yesterday?
c) How many presents did you get on your birthday?
d) How much time did you spend studying English at the weekend?
e) How many times did you go skiing last year?
f) How much fruit did you eat at your last meal?
g) How many phone calls did you make yesterday?

57

An American life
1809 He was born in Kentucky, USA and grew up in a poor family.
1818 His mother died.
1832 He wanted to study law but he didn't get a place at college.
1833 He started a business, but it wasn't successful.
1835 He got engaged to be married, but his fiancée died.
1836 He was ill and stayed in bed for six months.
1842 He got married to Mary Todd. They had four children, but only one survived.
1838 to 1859 He worked in politics but he lost eight elections.
1860 He became the 16th President of the United States.
1865 An actor, John Booth, shot and killed him at Ford's Theatre in Washington.
His name? Abraham Lincoln.

58

We had a delicious meal last weekend – on Friday night. It was my brother's 18th birthday, and the whole family went out. We had the meal in an Italian restaurant. It's called Mario's, and they do fantastic pizzas there – the best in town. There were fifteen of us – me, my brother, our parents, our grandmother, our cousins and my brother's best friends. I sat next to my grandmother, but she fell asleep after two glasses of wine. We all had pizza. Some people drank wine – including me – and the younger ones drank coke. The restaurant made my brother a special birthday cake and we all sang Happy Birthday – I think he was a bit embarrassed. The cake was delicious, and we had some champagne too. I think we stayed in the restaurant for nearly three hours. I didn't get home till 1am. It was a really good evening.

Unit 11

59

Albert is Jem's father. They've got the same smile.
Simon is Nancy's father. They've got the same mouth.
Sue is Will's mother. Will looks like Sue.
Belen is Carla's mother. They've got the same nose.
Gus and Zainab are brother and sister. They've got the same dark eyes.

60

(I = Interviewer; S = Stuart)
I: Stuart, you really like buying clothes, don't you?
S: Oh yes, I love it.
I: How many items of clothing have you got?
S: Well … I've got 350 shirts. I wear three or four different shirts every day.
I: Goodness … Er … Who does the washing?
S: My wife does the washing, and I do the ironing. Then I've got 200 suits. I like bright colours – red, blue, green.
I: Mm, I see.
S: Then I've got 150 pairs of trousers and 125 pairs of shoes.
I: Stuart, why have you got so many clothes?
S: Well, it's my hobby. Some people spend thousands of euros on cars, or holidays. I haven't got a car, and I never go on holiday. I buy clothes.

61

(See page 48.)

62

Conversation a
A: How many hats have you got?
B: Fourteen.
A: Forty?
B: No, fourteen.
A: Oh, fourteen.

Conversation b
A: How many ties have you got?
B: Nineteen.
A: Ninety?
B: No, nineteen.
A: Oh, nineteen.

Conversation c
A: How many rings have you got?
B: Fifteen.
A: Fifty?
B: No, fifteen.
A: Oh, fifteen.

Conversation d
A: How many T-shirts have you got?
B: Thirty.
A: Thirty?
B: Yes, thirty.
A: Oh, right.

63

Good evening. I'm Ross White and I'm standing outside Hollywood Theatre and I'm waiting for the big stars to arrive for this year's Oscar ceremony.

And here comes Penelope Jones. She's wearing a beautiful blue dress.

Oh, wow – there's Melanie Matthews. She's getting out of her car now – she's wearing a very short dress. Yes, very nice.

Er oh, here's Kerry Fisher. She's wearing a white suit and red boots. What's she doing? Oh, she's waving to her fans. That's nice. Such a big star, but she loves her fans.

Bobby Finn is arriving now. Oh, he's so good-looking! And who is that woman? He's holding her hand. She's lovely – she's wearing a long white dress.

64

a)
'Are you wearing jeans?'
'Yes, I am.'
'No, I'm not.'

b)
'Are you sitting next to a window?'
'Yes, I am.'
'No, I'm not.'

c)
'Is your teacher standing up?'
'Yes, she is.'
'No, she isn't.'

d)
'Is the traffic making a noise?'
'Yes, it is.'
'No, it isn't.'

e)
'Are the birds singing outside?'
'Yes, they are.'
'No, they aren't.'

f)
'Are you having a good time?'
'Yes, I am.'
'No, I'm not.'

Unit 12

◻ 65

About eight weeks after she made her dream book, Glenna was driving down a California freeway. Suddenly a gorgeous red and white Cadillac passed her. She looked at the car because it was a beautiful car. And the driver looked at her and smiled, and she smiled back. He followed her for the next fifteen miles. He parked, she parked … and eventually she married him.

After their first date, Jim sent Glenna a dozen roses. They dated for two years, and every Monday morning she received a red rose.

Then she found out that Jim had a hobby. His hobby was collecting diamonds.

They had the traditional wedding Glenna wanted, and Jim chose their honeymoon destination – it was St John's Island in the Caribbean. Then they moved into their beautiful new home.

Glenna didn't tell Jim about the dream book for almost a year after they got married.

Eight months after she created her dream book, Glenna became vice-president of human resources in the company where she worked – it was her dream job.

This sounds like a fairy tale, but it's a true story.

◻ 66

1

A: Next question. On the border of which two South American countries can you find the Iguaçu Falls?
B: Oh. Um. Mm, I know this one. Is it Argentina and Chile? No – Argentina and Brazil.
A: Is that your final answer?
B: Yes.
A: Are you sure?
B: Um, yes.
A: Carol, I asked you where you can find the Iguaçu Falls. Your answer was on the border of Argentina and Brazil. It's the correct answer. You've just won 125,000 euros!!!

2

Plenty of sunshine around today. Temperatures up to 32 degrees. And tomorrow is going to be another beautiful day. There may be some cloud in the north-east, but generally a warm and sunny day.

3

That's it. They've done it. Liverpool have beaten Real Madrid 3–2. A goal by Owen in the dying seconds … Incredible scenes here …

4

Police arrested two men after they attempted to rob a bank in the centre of London this morning. The men were armed, but nobody was hurt.

5

A: Oh hello, Mrs Jones. How are you today?
B: Oh, can't complain. Here, have you heard about that Andy Clifford?
A: No, what?
B: Well, I've heard he's going to get married to Rachel Smedley.
A: Rachel Smedley – no!

6

A: Well, Michael, you've had a very successful career in the film business. Did you always want to be a movie star?
B: Not exactly. I grew up on a farm in the Mid-West, and when I was a young boy all I wanted to be was a farmer like my dad.
A: So what made you change your mind?
B: Well, it was …

7

The shark is the king of the sea. It fills people with fear. But that's not the whole story. Yes, some kinds of shark are dangerous, but most of them are harmless and shy. Take the Spotted Wobbegong – not a beautiful specimen – quite ugly in fact …

8

A: Anybody want a cup of tea?
B: Yeah, okay.
Big Brother: This is Big Brother. Will Lynne please come to the Diary room immediately?
B: Ooh, I wonder what that's all about then?
A: Dunno. Do you want sugar in your tea?

◻ 67

(D = Danielle; L = Lynne)
D: Lynne, congratulations. How do you feel?
L: Oh, great. I feel fantastic. I'm so happy.
D: What's the first thing you're going to do when you get out?
L: I'm going to have a big party for all my friends. I missed them so much.
D: Ah. What are you going to do with the money?
L: Well, I'm going to give some of it to charity, and with the rest I'm going to buy a house for my mum.
D: So, which of your *Big Brother* housemates are you going to see again?
L: There are some people I'd like to see again, and there are two people I'm definitely not going to see again. I think you know who they are.
D: Yes, of course. That was really horrible. But your hair looks okay now.
L: Yeah, well …
D: Anyway Lynne, the question everyone wants to ask. You and Eddie became really good – er – friends in the House. So are you going to see Eddie again?
L: Well, I don't know. Yes, of course we're going to *see* one another. But we don't know what's going to happen.
D: What advice would you give to future *Big Brother* contestants?
L: Don't do it! No, I'm only joking. Be yourself, and be patient. It's very boring in there.
D: Finally, Lynne, what are your future plans?
L: Well, first I'm going to go out and spend some money. Then I want to start my singing career. I'm going to record a CD. Actually, I'd quite like to be a television presenter.
D: Oh – well, good luck.

◻ 68

(See page 53.)

◻ 69

(See page 53.)

Unit 13

◻ 70

(LPO = Lost property officer; J = Judy)
LPO: Lost property. How can I help?
J: Oh, um, hello … I'm ringing because I lost my bag yesterday.
LPO: I see. Well, we received thirty-eight bags yesterday. What colour is it and what's it made of?
J: Oh yes, er … It's black and it's made of leather.
LPO: Hm … black … leather … I've got twenty-four black leather bags here. Can you give me some more information?
J: Oh dear. Yes. Um, it's got a zip on the front and a long strap.
LPO: Has it got any pockets on the front?
J: No, but there's a pocket on the side for a mobile phone.
LPO: Okay, how big is it?
J: It's quite big – I wear it over my shoulder.
LPO: So what kind of bag is it? A shoulder bag?
J: Yes, a shoulder bag. That's right.
LPO: Is there anything in it?
J: Yes, there's an address book, and some keys. Oh, and Hissy.
LPO: Hissy?
J: Yes, Hissy the snake.
LPO: There's a snake … in your bag?
J: Yes, but don't worry, it's made of plastic. It belongs to my five-year-old son.
LPO: Right, well I think we have your bag here. The office is open from nine in the morning …

◻ 71

Think about the last time you went shopping.
Where and when did you go shopping?
What did you want to buy?
How long did you spend shopping?
Did you get what you wanted?
How much money did you spend and how did you pay?
Did you enjoy your shopping trip?

72

(See page 56.)

73

a) Sixty-six thousand, one hundred and twelve.
b) One hundred and ninety-four thousand, four hundred and fifty-nine.
c) Twenty-five thousand.
d) One hundred and fifty-seven thousand, nine hundred and forty-seven.
e) One million, nine hundred and eighteen thousand, three hundred and eighty-seven.
f) Three hundred and twenty-four thousand, one hundred and eighty-eight.

74

1 The most valuable bikini was valued at $194,459. The hand-made, diamond-encrusted bikini was made for Windsor fashion week in 2000.
2 The most valuable watch was in 18-carat gold made by Patek Phillippe in 1922. A Middle Eastern collector bought it for $1,918,387 in 1999.
3 Levi Strauss and Co. bought a 100-year-old pair of Levi 501s from a private collector for $25,000 in 1997.
4 The dress that Judy Garland wore in the 1939 production of *The Wizard of Oz* was auctioned for $324,188 in 1999.
5 The owner of the Las Vegas Hard Rock Hotel bought Geri Halliwell's Union Jack dress for $66,112 in 1998. She wore it for a Spice Girls' performance at the 1997 Brit Awards.
6 The boxing robe Mohammed Ali wore before his so-called 'Rumble in the Jungle' fight with George Foreman in 1974 was sold for $157,947 in a 1997 Beverly Hills sale.

Unit 14

75

(See page 58.)

76

a) Bend your knees.
b) Cross your legs.
c) Fold your arms.
d) Nod your head.
e) Clap your hands.
f) Stamp your feet.
g) Click your fingers.
h) Shrug your shoulders.

77

(See page 60.)

78

(D = Danny; L = Louise)
D: Do you want to come to the gym later?
L: Oh, no thanks. I can't. I'm too tired.
D: Well, you should do some exercise. Exercise gives you more energy.
L: It's not just that – I've got too much work. And I've got a bad back.
D: That's because you sit at your computer all day. You should go swimming – swimming is really good for your back.
L: I hate swimming – the swimming pool is too crowded – and anyway, I've got a cold.
D: A cold? Oh dear. Maybe you should go away for a few days.
L: Yes, I know, but I haven't got enough money to go away.
D: Look, you seem really fed up. Do you want to go out tomorrow night. We can go clubbing.
L: No, I can't go dancing. I've got a bad foot.
D: Too tired? A bad back? A cold? And a bad foot! Oh dear! I think you need a new body.

Unit 15

79

A: camera, curly, island, lovely, neighbour, selfish, stomach
B: alcohol, dominant, exercise, favourite, generous, jewellery
C: appointments, collector, contestant, impulsive, performance, successful

80

Think about someone you think is good-looking. It can be someone you know or a famous person.
What's his or her name?
What does he or she do?
How old is he or she?
What colour hair has he or she got?
What style is it?
What colour eyes has he or she got?
What other features has he or she got?
What sort of clothes does he or she wear?
What do you think he or she is doing now?

81

(See page 65.)

Unit 16

82

(T = Tom; M = Mum)
T: Hello.
M: Hello, Tom.
T: Oh hi, Mum. Are you okay?
M: Fine, thanks. But I need some help with my new computer.
T: Ah – do you want to surf the net?
M: No, I just want to send an email to Carol.
T: Okay. That's no problem. First, find the email icon.
M: Icon? What's an icon?
T: It's a little picture, like a symbol.
M: Where is it?
T: It's on your desktop.
M: Well, there's nothing on my desk,
T: No – Mum – your desktop is on your computer screen.
M: Oh. Well, I can see lots of little pictures there.
T: Right. You need to click on the email icon.
M: Click?
T: Press the button on your mouse.
M: Mouse?
T: THE THING IN YOUR HAND.
M: Oh, yes. Okay, I've done that.
T: Now, click on the new message icon and type Carol's email address in the box which says 'to'.
M: Okay.
T: Then type your message in the box and phone me back.
M: Okay. Bye.

83

(T = Tom/Thomas; M = Mum)
T: Yes, hello, Mum.
M: I'm ready to send that email.
T: Okay. To send the message, you need to go online.
M: Online?
T: Yes, you need to connect to the internet.
M: Ah yes. I knew that.
T: Now at the top of your screen there's a toolbar. Click on the 'Send and receive' icon, and this will connect you to the net through your modem.
M: Oh, Thomas, speak English! I don't understand computer language.
T: Oh, I don't believe this. Okay, what can you see at the top of your screen?
M: Well, there are lots of little pictures and …

84

(D = Darren; G = Geoff)
D: Geoff?
G: Darren! Wow, you haven't changed at all.
D: And you look exactly the same – good to see you.
G: Wow, I can't believe it – after fifteen years.
D: Yeah. Have you heard from any other old classmates?
G: Yes, a couple of people – that Friends Reunited website is brilliant.

D: Hey, have you got that list?

G: Yes, here it is.

D: Oh yes, I remember. '10 things to do before we're 30.' Well, we're 29 – how many things have *you* done?

G: Not many – three, I think. I've been snowboarding, and I've done a bungee jump, and I've visited John Lennon's grave in New York. And that's it really. What about you?

D: Let's see – I haven't recorded a CD – I stopped playing music when I left school.

G: Yeah, me too.

D: And I've been to a U2 concert but I haven't met them.

G: Have you travelled much?

D: Well, I've been to South America three times.

G: Wow!

D: But I haven't been to the Himalayas yet, or Egypt.

G: Have you ever been snowboarding?

D: Yes, I've done that. But I haven't done a bungee jump. I haven't made a lot of money either – I'm a teacher!

G: Well, I've made a lot of money, but I've spent it. Anyway, have you met the love of your life?

D: No, I haven't met anyone special yet. How about you?

G: Yes, I forgot to tell you. I'm married to Pamela.

D: Pamela?

G: Yes, you know, the gorgeous singer in our band.

85

a)
'Have you ever visited the website for your old school?'
'Yes, I have.'
'No, I haven't.'

b)
'Has your school ever tried to get in touch with you?'
'Yes, it has.'
'No, it hasn't.'

c)
'Have you ever been to a reunion at your school?'
'Yes, I have.'
'No, I haven't.'

d)
'Have you ever received an email from an old friend?'
'Yes, I have.'
'No, I haven't.'

e)
'Have your parents ever sent you an email?'
'Yes, they have.'
'No, they haven't.'

f)
'Have you ever met somebody new on the internet?'
'Yes, I have.'
'No, I haven't.'

86

Think about an old school friend you would like to get in touch with.
What's his or her name?
Where did you first meet?
How old were you?
Why did you become friends?
What sort of things did you talk about?
What sort of things did you do together?
What is your best memory of him or her?
When was the last time you saw him or her?
What do you think he or she is doing now?
Why would you like to get in touch with him or her?

Unit 17

87

(P = Presenter; M1, 2, 3 = Men; W1, 2, 3 = Women)

P: This is City Radio. My name is Andy Cowle. Earlier, we asked people in the street, 'What drives you mad on the road?' Here are some of their answers.

1
M1: I can't stand it when people drive very slowly. They usually go out at the weekend, and drive very slowly on country roads where it's impossible to overtake them.

2
W1: I hate it when people park their cars on the pavement. The road is for cars – the pavement is for pedestrians!

3
M2: I hate it when drivers indicate to turn left … and turn right! … or go straight on! It's so dangerous!

4
W2: Well, I don't like getting stuck in traffic jams. In my city, the rush hour in the morning, and in the evening, is awful. I try to work at home as much as possible.

5
M3: Road works drive me mad, especially on the motorway. You go on the motorway to save time, and then you get stuck in a traffic jam because of the road works.

6
W3: It drives me mad when people use their mobile phones in the car. I nearly had an accident last week because this woman was talking on her phone and she didn't see the traffic lights turn red. She nearly killed me.

88

first, second, third, fourth, fifth, sixth, seventh, eighth, ninth, tenth

89

1   Your starting point is A1. Go straight on, take the third right, the second left, and go straight on. Where are you?

2   Your starting point is A2. Take the first left, the first right, the fifth right, and the first left. Where are you?

3   Your starting point is A3. Go straight on, take the fourth left, the second right, and go straight on. Where are you?

Unit 18

90

(See page 76.)

91

a)
'Were you living in the same house this time last year?'
'Yes, I was.'
'No, I wasn't.'

b)
'Were your parents watching TV at 11.30 last night?
'Yes, they were.'
'No, they weren't.'

c)
'Were you having an English lesson this time yesterday?'
'Yes, I was.'
'No, I wasn't.'

d)
'Was it raining when you woke up this morning?'
'Yes, it was.'
'No, it wasn't.'

e)
'Were you wearing a hat when you went out this morning?'
'Yes, I was.'
'No, I wasn't.'

f)
'Were you speaking English when the lesson started?'
'Yes, I was.'
'No, I wasn't.'

92

The princess and the frog
Have you ever heard the story of the princess and the frog?

Well, once upon a time, there was a princess. She was beautiful, confident and independent.

She lived in a castle in a country far away.

One day, she was sitting near a pond in the grounds of her castle. She was thinking about her life.

There she met a frog.

The frog said to her, 'Beautiful princess, I was once a handsome prince. But then an evil witch changed me into a frog. Kiss me and I will turn back into a handsome, young prince. Then, my darling, we can get married and live in your castle with my mother. You can prepare my meals, wash my clothes and look after my children.'

Later, as the princess was enjoying a meal of frog's legs in a delicious cream sauce, she smiled and thought to herself, 'Thanks, my prince … but no, thanks.'

Unit 19

🔈 **93, 94, 95**

(See page 78.)

🔈 **96**

a)
'Was your house built before 1980?'
'Yes, it was.'
'No, it wasn't.'

b)
'Were your shoes designed in Italy?'
'Yes, they were.'
'No, they weren't.'

c)
'Is your salary paid by cheque?'
'Yes, it is.'
'No, it isn't.'

d)
'Were you invited to any parties last week?'
'Yes, I was.'
'No, I wasn't.'

e)
'Is your name spelt the same way in English?'
'Yes, it is.'
'No, it isn't.'

f)
'Was your mobile phone made in Japan?'
'Yes, it was.'
'No, it wasn't.'

🔈 **97**

London in winter
Today will start off very wet with temperatures of 9 or 10 degrees Celsius.

It will be cloudy in the afternoon, and there will probably be rain later on. It will be dull all day.

Tomorrow will be the same, and the next day, and the day after.

Summer might be a bit sunnier, but not much.

🔈 **98**

I like October. It's autumn in Japan. Yes, autumn is my favourite time of year. In Kyoto the weather is beautiful in October. It's warm, but not hot. In summer it's too hot – I hate it – but in October, the temperature is perfect.

Also, the countryside is very colourful at that time of year. The trees are red and orange. We have a name for this in Japan – it's called 'koyo' – it means the changing colour of the trees in autumn. I usually wear light clothes – T-shirts and dresses. You don't need a coat when you go out. It's lovely.

Of course October is not holiday time, but at the weekend we go for walks in the hills and we have picnics. We enjoy looking at the countryside at that time of year.

I like that time of year because it's beautiful. Yes, I think Kyoto is the best place in the world at that time of year.

Unit 20

🔈 **99**

(See page 82)

🔈 **100**

And here are the words for tonight's bingo.
meant, meant   caught, caught
slept, slept   worn, worn   made, made
woken, woken   done, done
brought, brought   shot, shot   had, had
spent, spent   paid, paid   kept, kept
felt, felt   broken, broken   fallen, fallen
thought, thought   found, found
lent, lent   spoken, spoken   eaten, eaten
written, written   sat, sat   met, met
taught, taught   read, read   heard, heard
driven, driven   sold, sold   built, built

🔈 **101**

A Hollywood director was filming an important film in the desert when an old Native American man came up to him and said, 'Tomorrow rain.'

The next day it rained.

A few days later, the director was talking to the cameraman about the next day's filming. The Native American went up to him and said, 'Tomorrow storm.'

He was right again, and he saved the director thousands of dollars.

The director was very impressed and gave the old man a job.

The old man continued to predict the weather correctly, but then he didn't come for three weeks.

The director was planning to film an important scene and he needed good weather. So he went to look for the Native American.

When he found the old man, he said,
'Listen, I have to film an important scene tomorrow. What will the weather be like?'

The old man shook his head and said, 'Don't know. Radio broken.'

🔈 **102**

Think about a journey that you did many times when you were younger.
Where did your journey start and finish?
How far was it?
How did you travel?
What time did you usually set off?
How long did it take you?
What sort of countryside did you go through?
What sort of buildings did you go past?
Who did you usually travel with?
What did you usually do on your journey?
When was the last time you did this journey?

Macmillan Education
Between Towns Road, Oxford OX4 3PP
A division of Macmillan Publishers Limited
Companies and representatives throughout the world

ISBN 0 333 92440 1

Text © Sue Kay and Vaughan Jones 2003
Design and illustration © Macmillan Publishers Limited 2003

First published 2003

Project management by Desmond O'Sullivan, ELT Publishing Services.
Designed by Jackie Hill, 320 Design.
Illustrated by Cyrus Deboo pp20, 71, 72(b), 81; Rebecca Halls pp44, 45,
84, 85; Monica Laita p11(t); Ed McLachlan pp15, 24, 29, 36, 40, 42, 61,
63, 64, 69, 72(t), 73, 75, 76, 77, 82, 83, 95, 96; Gavin Reece at New
Division pp4, 5, 9, 11(b), 12, 14, 39, 49, 54, 74, 90, 97, 102; Kim Williams
pp13, 30, 43.
Cover design by Andrew Oliver.
Cover painting Patrick in Italy © Howard Hodgkin.

Authors' acknowledgements
We would like to thank all our students and colleagues at the
following institutions where, with their help, we were able to try out
our ideas in the classroom and throw out anything that didn't work:
Susan Barber at the Lake School, Oxford; Ingrid Widdows and Steve
Haysham at the Oxford College of Further Education; Faith Pritchard at
Campsfield House, Oxford; Ceri Jones and Elizabeth Cowin at
International House, Madrid. Also, all our friends and colleagues in the
various Escuelas Oficiales de Idiomas in Spain that we visited or taught
in, particularly Alejandro Zarzalejo and Araceli García Tubio at the EOI
Las Rozas, María José Pi at the EOI Quart de Poblet, and Marisa de Dios
at the EOI Valencia. A big thankyou to Mick Quirke and Manolo
Grijalvo of Macmillan Heinemann Spain for organising our teaching
posts in Spain.
We are especially grateful to Philip Kerr for the Inside Out Workbook
and to Ceri Jones for her contribution, to Helena Gomm and John Hird
for the Inside Out Teacher's Book, to Pete Maggs for the highly
successful weekly Inside Out e-lessons (now over 40,000 subscribers), to
Guy Jackson for running the Inside Out website at www.insideout.net,
and to everybody involved in the Inside Out Resource Pack – a great
team!
At Macmillan Education, we would like to thank Sue Bale (publishing
director) and David Riley (publisher). We would also like to thank Pippa
McNee (freelance picture researcher), Alyson Maskell and Celia
Bingham (freelance editors), Paulette McKean (freelance permissions
editor), Xanthe Sturt Taylor (freelance phonetics writer), as well as
James Richardson and Vince Cross (freelance audio producers), and last
but not least Jackie Hill – our wonderfully talented freelance designer.
Many thanks also go to the Macmillan production and marketing
teams who have worked so hard to make Inside Out what it is.
As Inside Out Elementary marks the end of the Inside Out project (for
the moment!), we reluctantly take leave of Des O'Sullivan, (freelance
project manager). Over the past three and a half years that we have
been working together, we have enjoyed and benefited from Des's
humour, sensitivity, energy, drive and sheer professionalism. We cannot
speak highly enough of him – it has been a privilege to work with him,
and we have learned a great deal from the experience. Much more
than that, Des has supported us through all the ups and downs of work
and life throughout the Inside Out project, often in ways that go
beyond the call of duty. Thanks, Des, we couldn't have done it without
you and we look forward to working with you again in the future.
We would like to give a special thankyou to Michael Rundell who took
time from his busy schedule to provide us with the necessary data from
the Macmillan Essential Dictionary to inform our Wordlist.
We would also like to thank Chris Campbell and Simon Dix (The Swan
School, Oxford), Jenny Johnson (International House, Barcelona) and
Beth Neher (Hammersmith and West London College) for their
insightful comments which have helped to make this a better book.
Finally, we are so grateful to our families for their ongoing support and
understanding.

This book, along with all the books in the Inside Out series, is
dedicated to Mike Esplen – former managing director of Heinemann
ELT. Thank you, Mike, for believing in us during those crucial early
stages and giving us enough time and space to develop our ideas.

The authors and publishers would like to thank the following for
permission to reproduce their material:
She's Got You Words and Music by Hank Cochran copyright © Sony/ATV
Acuff Rose Music 1971, reprinted by permission of Sony/ATV Music
Publishing. I Have a Dream Words and Music by B Andersson/B Ulvaeus,
reprinted by permission of Bocu Music Ltd. Extract and photograph
from 'Letter From Karyn …' from www.savekaryn.com, reprinted by
permission of the author. John Kitching 'I Love Geography' copyright ©
John Kitching 2002 from The Works 2 edited by Brian Moses and Pie
Corbett (Macmillan, 2002), reprinted by permission of the author.
Whilst every effort has been made to trace owners of copyright
material in this book, there may have been some cases when the
publishers have been unable to contact the owners. We should be
grateful to hear from anyone who recognises copyright material and
who is unacknowledged. We shall be pleased to make the necessary
amendments in future editions of the book.

The authors and publishers wish to thank the following for permission
to reproduce their photographs:
Alamy pp18(tr), 34 (fishing), 50(c, d), 66, 78(l); All Action p18(tl); All
Sport p34 (swimming); Roderick Angle Photography p48; Anglia / Bob
Hobbs p47; Axiom p16(l); www.savekaryn.com p55; Jay Conely p68(l);
Corbis pp9, 18(m), 21, 22(a), 28(tl, r), 34 (scuba diving), 37, 41(l), 57, 58,
62, 70(l), 78(3), 79(m, t), 80; Corbis / Sygma pp14, 16(r), 28(ml); 4C's
Enterprises p70(b); Rob Fitzpatrick p68(rt); FriendsReunited.com p67;
Tim Friers p68(rb); Image Bank pp17(r), 21(b), 22(c), 27, 50(b, e, g); Sue
Kay and Vaughan Jones p46; Music Pics p50; Antonio Olmos p31;
O'Neill p35; P.A News p8; Photodisc pp88, 100; Photographers Choice
p34 (surfing); Photonica Green p66; Rex Features pp39(r), 96, 99; Stone
pp22(b), 32(t), 34 (sailing, windsurfing, rowing), 50(a, f), 60, 61, 81,
70(r), 78 (2, 4); Tait family p10; Taxi p17(l), 32(b), 34 (canoeing, kite
surfing); Elizabeth Whiting Associates pp19, 87.

Commissioned photography by Haddon Davies pp6, 7, 26, 38, 52.
Models provided by Elliot Brown and The Source Model agencies
Oxford.
Thanks to The White Horse Sports and Tennis Centre, Abingdon.
Researched images sourced by Pippa McNee Picture Research.

Printed and bound in Spain by Edelvives SA.
2007 2006 2005 2004 2003
10 9 8 7 6 5 4 3 2 1